COMPLETE EnglishSmart®

GRADE 7

Grade

Contents 7

Dear Parent,

Thank you for choosing our *Complete EnglishSmart* as your child's learning companion.

We are confident that *Complete EnglishSmart* is the ultimate supplementary workbook your child needs to build his or her English language skills.

Complete EnglishSmart explores the fundamental aspects of language development – listening comprehension, grammar, reading, and writing – by introducing each concept with an easy-to-understand definition and clear examples. This is followed by a variety of interesting activities to provide plenty of practice for your child. There is also a note box at the end of each unit for your child to note down what he or she has learned.

To further ensure that your child retains the language concepts and enjoys the material, there is a review at the end of each section and a Creative Corner section at the end of the book to help your child consolidate the language concepts in a fun and meaningful way. The accompanying online audio clips (www.popularbook.ca/downloadcentre) let your child practise and develop his or her listening skills.

We hope that your child will have fun learning and developing his or her English language skills with our *Complete EnglishSmart*.

Your Partner in Education,
Popular Book Company (Canada) Limited

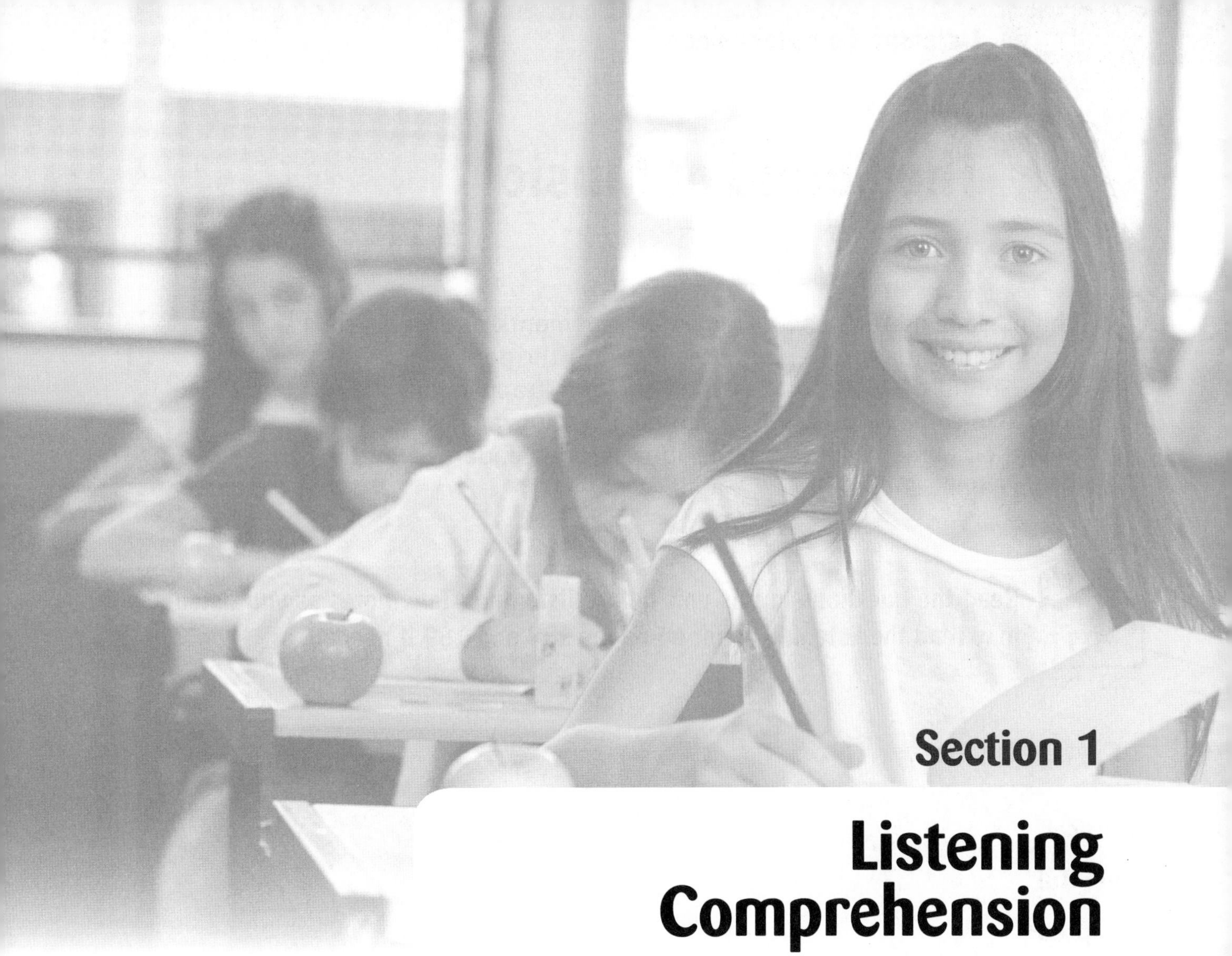

Section 1

Listening Comprehension

Scan this QR Code or go to Download Centre at **www.popularbook.ca** for audio clips.

UNIT 1

The Sound of Music

This passage narrates the struggles, achievements, and legacy of Georg and Maria von Trapp. It describes how the popular musical "The Sound of Music" is based on the von Trapp family, how they overcame adversity by becoming a musical group, and how their names still live on through their descendants and the Trapp Family Lodge.

Read the questions in this unit before listening. Take notes as you listen. You may read the listening script on pages 188 and 189 if needed.

Keywords

musical
eventful
adapted
Broadway
starring
Austria
decorated
scarlet fever
abbey
fortune
Great Depression
annexed
emigrated
ski lodge
attraction
accomplished

Notes

A. Read the questions. Then check the correct answers.

1. Who starred in the musical "The Sound of Music"?
   - (A) Maria and Georg von Trapp
   - (B) Julie Andrews and Georg von Trapp
   - (C) Julie Andrews and Christopher Plummer
   - (D) Julie Andrews and Maria von Trapp

2. How did the family flee from Austria?
   - (A) by forming a musical group
   - (B) by train
   - (C) by settling in Vermont
   - (D) by emigrating to the United States

3. How many children were in the family's musical group?
   - (A) three
   - (B) five
   - (C) seven
   - (D) ten

4. Who managed the family lodge after Georg and Maria passed away?
   - (A) their son Rodgers
   - (B) their grandson Johannes
   - (C) their son George
   - (D) their son Johannes

B. Listen to the questions and answer options. Then write the correct letters in the boxes.

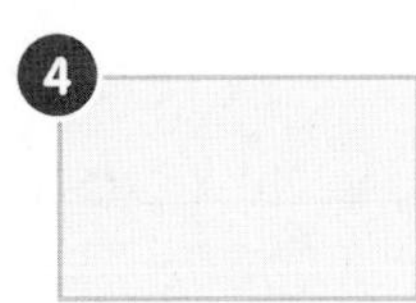

C. Write "T" for the true statements and "F" for the false ones.

1. Captain von Trapp married a woman named Agathe Whitehead. ______
2. Maria von Trapp died of scarlet fever. ______
3. Georg and Maria von Trapp had seven children together. ______
4. The Trapp Family Singers sang all over Europe. ______
5. In the United States, the family settled in Venice. ______
6. The Trapp Family Lodge includes 2500 acres of property. ______

D. Answer the questions.

1. Describe Captain von Trapp's life before he married Maria Augusta Kutschera.

____

____

____

2. Explain how the von Trapp family dealt with the following:

(A) The Great Depression: ______________________________

____

(B) Hitler's annexation of Austria: ______________________________

____

3. What is the legacy of Georg and Maria von Trapp?

____

____

____

____

E. Listen to the passage "The Sound of Music" again. Then write a summary in no more than 120 words.

1.1

Include only the main points in the summary. Use your own words.

Summary

My Notes

UNIT 2

So You Want to Be an Author

This passage explains new ways for aspiring authors to publish their books and the reasons why they want to have their works published. You will also learn about the current plight of brick-and-mortar bookstores.

Read the questions in this unit before listening. Take notes as you listen. You may read the listening script on pages 190 and 191 if needed.

Keywords

book-signing
published
agent
manuscript
print run
accessible
desktop publishing
print-on-demand
warehousing
distribution
marketing
channel
brick-and-mortar
promotional
mandatory
phenomenon

Notes

A. Read the questions. Then check the correct answers.

1. Who usually offers courses on book publishing?

   (A) agents
   (B) famous authors
   (C) publishers
   (D) little-known authors

2. What does POD stand for?

   (A) publish-on-demand
   (B) print-on-demand
   (C) print-on-desktop
   (D) photocopy-of-design

3. What overhead costs can POD publishing eliminate?

   (A) warehousing and distribution costs
   (B) marketing and printing costs
   (C) publishing and distribution costs
   (D) warehousing and marketing costs

KIM'S STORAGE **INVOICE**

Description	Amount
Storage – 10 pallets	$250
Delivery	$100
Labour	$50
Total	$400

4. What are some examples of subject matter that is narrow in scope mentioned in the passage?

   (A) local recipes and family memoirs
   (B) local histories and family memoirs
   (C) world histories and family recipes
   (D) local recipes and family recipes

B. Listen to the questions and answer options. Then write the correct letters in the boxes.

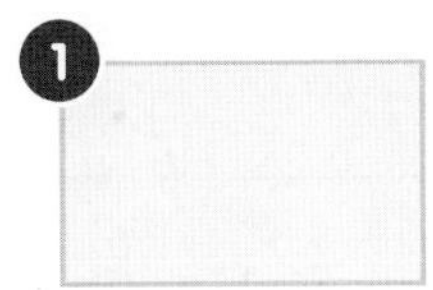

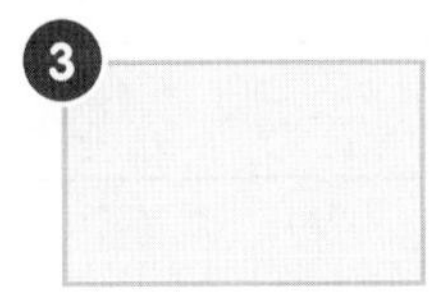

C. Fill in the blanks with the correct words from the passage.

1. So-called "agents" may simply ______________ and mail a writer's manuscript to ______________ .

2. The average writer will tell you that ______________ is not the motivating factor.

3. The author pays the costs of ______________ and a fee to the POD company to get his or her book published.

4. POD books are suitable for subject matter that is ______________ in scope.

5. These days, the challenge in becoming an author is in being able to ______________ the book once it is made.

6. Fewer books are being sold in ______________ bookstores nowadays.

7. An author needs to ______________ his or her book, which means establishing relationships with various organizations.

D. Answer the questions.

1. What are some of the motivating factors for writers who want to publish their books?

____

____

____

2. Explain how print-on-demand publishing eliminates overhead costs associated with warehousing and distribution.

____

____

____

E. **Listen to the passage "So You Want to Be an Author" again. Then write a summary in no more than 120 words.**

2.1

Include only the main points in the summary. Use your own words.

Summary

My Notes

UNIT 3 A Farewell to Pluto

This passage explains the history of both the inclusion of Pluto and the reasons for Pluto's removal as a planet. You will also learn about Pluto's current status as a "dwarf planet" and the public's reaction to Pluto losing its planet status.

Read the questions in this unit before listening. Take notes as you listen. You may read the listening script on pages 192 and 193 if needed.

Keywords

mnemonic

Pluto

classified

astronomer

Clyde Tombaugh

telescope

extremity

orbit

celestial

Hubble

stipulation

gravity

spherical

dwarf planet

Kuiper Belt

Notes

A. Read the questions. Then check the correct answers.

1. What did the mnemonic in the passage help people memorize?
   - (A) the names and colours of all the planets
   - (B) the names and sizes of all the planets
   - (C) the colours and order of all the planets
   - (D) the names and order of all the planets

2. Which organization declared that Pluto was no longer a planet?
   - (A) the National Aeronautics and Space Administration
   - (B) the National Astronomical Union
   - (C) the International Astronomical Union
   - (D) the International Aeronautical Union

3. Which is a stipulation of the redefined meaning of "planet"?
   - (A) It should be small enough.
   - (B) It should orbit the sun.
   - (C) It should have water.
   - (D) It should be a "dwarf planet".

4. What are the five "dwarf planets" in our solar system?
   - (A) Neptune, Ceres, Eris, Makemake, and Haumea
   - (B) Pluto, Ceres, Neptune, Mercury, and Haumea
   - (C) Pluto, Ceres, Eris, Makemake, and Haumea
   - (D) Pluto, Ceres, Neptune, Eris, and Haumea

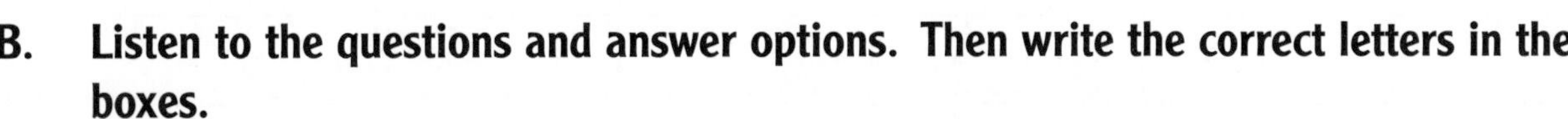

B. Listen to the questions and answer options. Then write the correct letters in the boxes.

C. Put the facts in order. Write the letters in the boxes.

A Telescope and space technology improved.

B The IAU redefined the meaning of "planet".

C Pluto was discovered.

D Pluto was reclassified as a "dwarf planet".

E It was found that a celestial body near Pluto is larger than Pluto.

D. Answer the questions.

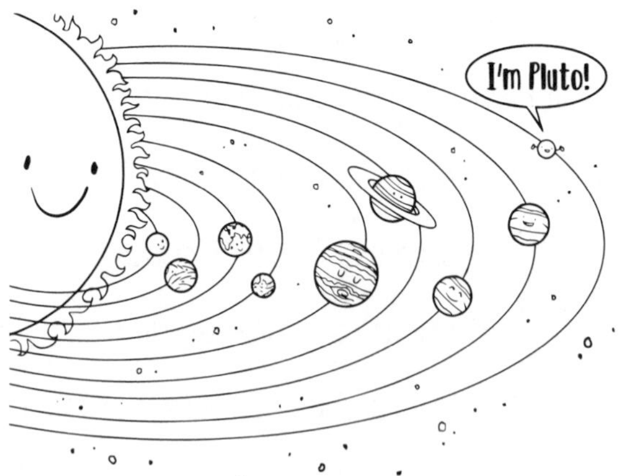

1. Why do you think astronomers had waited so long before declassifying Pluto as a planet?

____

2. What made the International Astronomical Union decide to take Pluto off the list of planets?

____

3. What is the redefined meaning of "planet"?

____

4. How did people react to the IAU's decision?

____

E. **Listen to the passage "A Farewell to Pluto" again. Then write a summary in no more than 120 words.**

Include only the main points in the summary. Use your own words.

Summary

My Notes

UNIT 4 The Facts behind the Figures

This passage teaches the facts behind some historical figures and how they earned their reputations. You will learn about Dracula, the Vandals, Johnny Appleseed, and Cleopatra.

Read the questions in this unit before listening. Take notes as you listen. You may read the listening script on pages 194 and 195 if needed.

Keywords

reputation
vampire
Romania
invade
Vandals
nomadic
Goths
Visigoths
Franks
capture
explore
Egyptian
empire
diplomat
Plutarch
conversationalist

Notes

A. Read the questions. Then check the correct answers.

1. What is the name of the vampire in Bram Stoker's book?

   (A) Count Dracula (B) Vlad Dracula
   (C) Vlad the Impaler (D) Dracula the Impaler

2. What was the name of the Vandal king?

   (A) King Goth
   (B) King Visigoth
   (C) King Gaiseric
   (D) King Frank

3. What were some of the things that John Chapman liked to do?

   (A) walk, explore, plant apple seeds, and spend time with nature
   (B) explore and destroy property
   (C) walk, explore, and fight with people who vandalized property
   (D) plant seeds, meet Native Americans, and fight invading armies

4. Where are the ancient coins with Cleopatra's images kept?

   (A) in Romania and Egypt
   (B) in Massachusetts
   (C) in England and Egypt
   (D) in Central Europe

B. Listen to the questions and answer options. Then write the correct letters in the boxes.

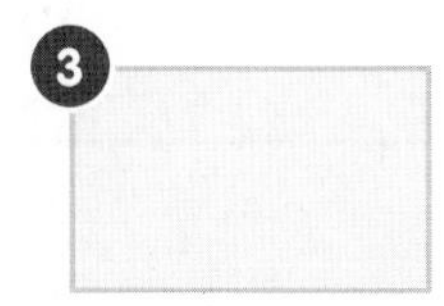

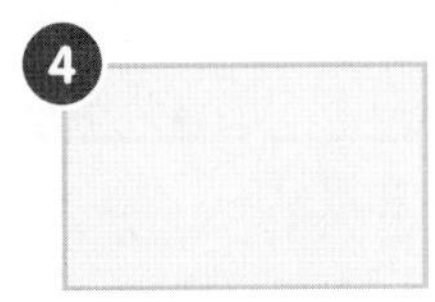

C. Check to show whether the following statements are true or false.

		True	False
1.	Vlad Dracula was a vampire.	○	○
2.	An Englishman named Bram Stoker wrote a book called *Dracula*.	○	○
3.	The Vandals were a tribe of people who destroyed property.	○	○
4.	Johnny Appleseed was just a storybook character.	○	○
5.	John Chapman walked around and explored Massachusetts for 50 years.	○	○
6.	Cleopatra was a skilful diplomat.	○	○

D. Answer the questions.

1. Why is Vlad Dracula known as a vampire?

2. Who were the Vandals?

3. What contributed to Cleopatra's reputation as the most beautiful woman in the world?

E. Listen to the passage "The Facts behind the Figures" again. Then write a summary in no more than 120 words.

4.1

Include only the main points in the summary. Use your own words.

Summary

My Notes

UNIT 5

The Art of Cubism

This passage explores how Cubism came about, and its evolution and influences. It tells you how it began as an idea by the artists Braque and Picasso, and how it permeated other forms of expression, including music, sculpting, and even literature.

Read the questions in this unit before listening. Take notes as you listen. You may read the listening script on pages 196 and 197 if needed.

Keywords

evolution

innovation

Cubism

influence

Georges Braque

Pablo Picasso

Impressionist

deconstruct

abstract

monochromatic

collage

avant-garde

composer

Igor Stravinsky

literature

Notes

A. Read the questions. Then check the correct answers.

1. When did the idea of Cubism come about?
   - (A) at the end of the 20th century
   - (B) in the middle of the 20th century
   - (C) at the beginning of the 20th century
   - (D) at the beginning of the 21st century

2. What are some characteristics of Impressionist art?
   - (A) monochromatic and dull colours
   - (B) three-dimensional images
   - (C) use of shapes and angles
   - (D) bright and vivid colours

3. What did Picasso experiment with in his paintings around 1912?
   - (A) wood and newspaper
   - (B) chair caning and metal
   - (C) wood and glass
   - (D) wood chips and iron

4. Put the appearances of the art forms in order from the earliest to the most recent.
   - (A) Cubism, Impressionism, Collage
   - (B) Impressionism, Collage, Cubism
   - (C) Cubism, Collage, Impressionism
   - (D) Impressionism, Cubism, Collage

B. Listen to the questions and answer options. Then write the correct letters in the boxes.

1 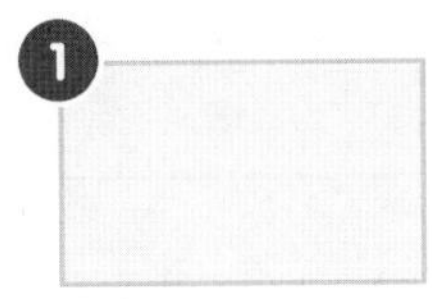

2 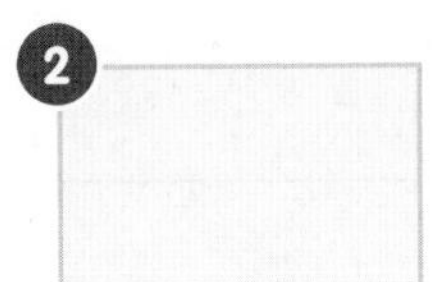

3 

4 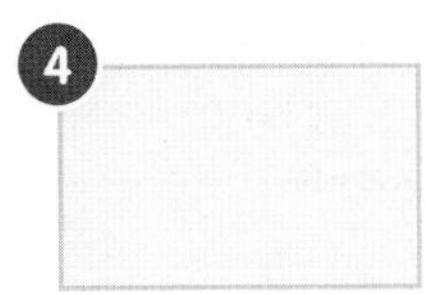

C. In point form, compare Impressionism and Cubism.

Impressionism

Cubism

D. Answer the questions.

1. How did the craft form called "collage" develop?

2. What are the characteristics of Cubist music?

3. What are some examples of Cubist literature?

4. In your opinion, which is more appealing, Impressionism or Cubism? Why?

E. **Listen to the passage "The Art of Cubism" again. Then write a summary in no more than 120 words.**

5.1

Include only the main points in the summary. Use your own words.

Summary

My Notes

Ikebana – The Peaceful Power of Flowers

This passage explores Ikebana – the Japanese art of flower arrangement. You will learn about the origins of Ikebana, some of the different schools of Ikebana, and the purpose of Ikebana. You will also learn about the various benefits of practising Ikebana.

Read the questions in this review before listening. Take notes as you listen. You may read the listening script on pages 198 and 199 if needed.

Notes

A. Circle the answers.

1. Indoor potted plants act as nature's ______ .

   pollutants

   air purifiers

   toxins

   mood

2. Flower arrangement is popular among those who believe that one's home is their ______ .

   school

   haven

   garden

   lives

3. Buddhist priests in ______ first developed the art of Ikebana.

   Japan

   China

   Korea

   both China and Korea

4. The Ikenobo school has ______ .

   an unbalanced sense of space

   a modern sense of space

   an asymmetrical sense of space

   a geometric sense of space

5. The Sogetsu school is more free-styling in terms of ______ .

   colour, materials, and size

   colour, materials, and symmetry

   colour, materials, and space

   materials, lines, and space

6. Ikebana is founded on the idea of the essential bond between ______ .

   human beings and ancient practices

   human beings and agriculture

   human beings and nature

   flowers and nature

7. Ikebana attempts to recreate the beauty of ______ .

   peace

   landscapes

   colour

   flowers

8. The act of focusing on creating a flower arrangement provides a sense of ______ .

   monotony

   tension

   dread

   calm

B. Listen to the questions and answer options. Then write the correct letters in the boxes.

C. Write "T" for the true statements and "F" for the false ones.

1. Ikebana began as a popular pastime. ____
2. Recreating the beauty of the outdoors is a way to replace nature in its many forms. ____
3. The act of growing and picking flowers is an integral part of Ikebana. ____
4. Expressing oneself through the beauty of flowers in nature can give great peace of mind. ____

D. Rewrite the statements so they are true.

1. Buddhism was introduced to Japan from China and Korea around the fifth century.

   ____

   ____

2. Ikebana is a popular pastime mainly among Japanese girls and women.

   ____

   ____

3. The Ikenobo school features a modern style of Ikebana.

   ____

   ____

4. Ikebana attempts to recreate the beauty of indoor flower arrangement and bring it outdoors.

   ____

   ____

E. Identify and write the schools of Ikebana based on the information provided. Then fill in the information.

- with a geometric sense of space
- uses imported plant types from when Japan opened its doors to the West
- free-styling in terms of colour, materials, and space

1. ____________________ School

Features:

- modern style
- ______________________________________

____

____

2. ____________________ School

Features:

- an offshoot of the Ikenobo School
- ______________________________________

____

____

3. ____________________ School

Features:

- classic school
- with clean and simple lines
- ______________________________________

____

____

F. **Fill in the blanks of this journal entry with the correct information.**

Monday, June 3, 2019

My First Attempt at Ikebana!

I have learned that flowers can do much to bring ❸ p________ and ❹ t________ to our lives, so today I delved into Ikebana – the Japanese art of ❺ f________ a________ .

❶ a p________

❷ bamboo f________

Before I went to buy the materials I needed, I planned out the colours and ideas for my design. I was inspired by the ❻ c________ , simple, and carefully considered lines of the Ikenobo school.

I incorporated bamboo fronds and a peony to recreate the groves and ❼ g________ found in outdoor ❽ l________ .

The act of ❾ f________ on creating this arrangement provided me with a great sense of ❿ c________ . I felt as if I were one with nature!

My first attempt at Ikebana was a success, and I feel like I have so much to gain from this ancient ⓫ a________ .

the receptacle in which I placed the flowers and plants

My finished arrangement!

G. Answer the questions.

1. Explain how Ikebana attempts to recreate the beauty of the outdoors.

2. How is Ikebana a spiritual endeavour?

R1.1

H. Listen to the passage "Ikebana – The Peaceful Power of Flowers" again. Then write a summary in no more than 120 words.

Listen carefully to make sure you catch all of the important points of the passage to include them in your summary. Use your own words.

Summary

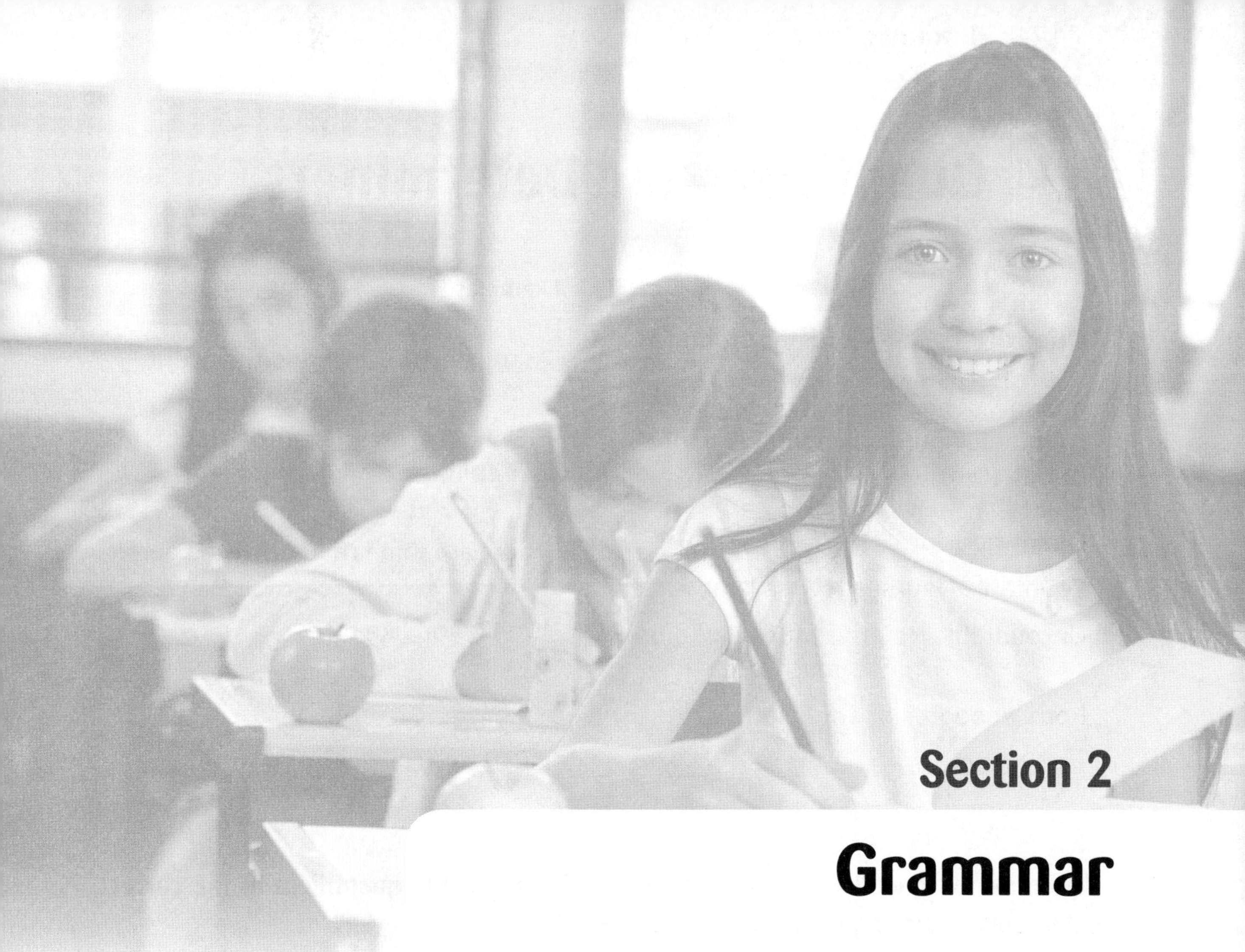

Section 2

Grammar

UNIT 1 Quantifiers and Determiners

Quantifiers are words and phrases that precede nouns to indicate quantity. They can be used to modify countable nouns, uncountable nouns, or both.

Quantifiers for

Countable Nouns: a few, several, etc.

Uncountable Nouns: a little bit of, not much, etc.

Both: enough, not any, a lot of, etc.

Examples

- Many people attended the event. (people ← countable noun)
- She had a great deal of doubt in her abilities. (doubt ← uncountable noun)
- There are some children at the park. (children ← countable noun)
- Would you like some sugar? (sugar ← uncountable noun)

A. Underline the quantifiers in the sentences. Then put the quantifiers in the correct categories by writing the sentence numbers.

1. They had a large number of blankets to build forts with.
2. A couple of houses on this lane are owned by Jane's father.
3. None of my siblings can attend my graduation.
4. I have a great deal of admiration for my teacher.
5. She had enough money to last her a lifetime!
6. There is some milk left in the carton.
7. All of her friends congratulated her.
8. There is not much honey left.
9. There were several options.
10. She held out a few coins.
11. A bit of luck is needed.
12. I have many books in my room.

Quantifiers Used for:	
Countable Nouns	Uncountable Nouns

"**Little**" and "**a little**" are quantifiers modifying uncountable nouns, whereas "**few**" and "**a few**" modify countable nouns.

Examples

- I had little choice in the matter.
- A little courtesy goes a long way.
- Few people realized the severity of the issue.
- Winnie still had a few candidates to consider.

B. Fill in the blanks with the correct quantifiers to complete the sentences.

little **a little** **few** **a few**

1. Josh has ______________ friends at school; he should socialize more.
2. The results will be announced in ______________ days.
3. Andrew and Jack had very ______________ money left after the shopping spree.
4. Could you please put ______________ oil in the pan?
5. Here are ______________ tips that you may find useful.
6. Cinderella's evil sisters gave her ______________ time to rest; they always kept her busy.
7. I have ______________ toys left from my childhood days. I still like to play with them.
8. There is still ______________ snow on the ground.
9. ______________ places in the world can compete with Canada's multiculturalism. It is one of the best countries!

Section 2 Grammar

Determiners are words that precede nouns and modify them. There are many different types of determiners: articles, possessive adjectives, demonstrative adjectives, and more.

Article	Possessive Adjective	Demonstrative Adjective
a, an, the	my, your, his, her, our, their	this, that, these, those

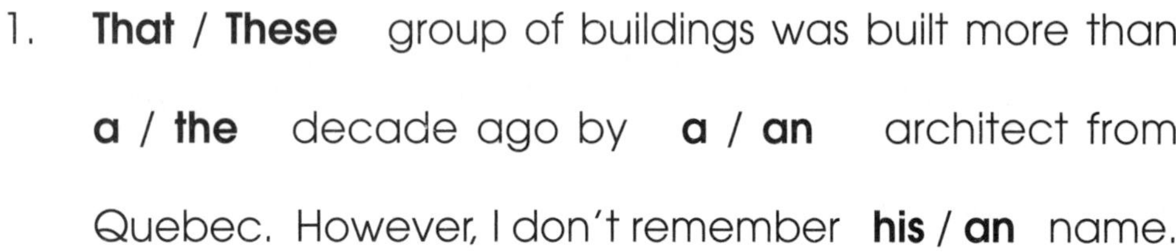

Examples

- An apple fell from the tree.
- Can I eat your apple?
- This apple tastes good.

C. Circle the correct determiners to complete the sentences.

1. **That / These** group of buildings was built more than **a / the** decade ago by **a / an** architect from Quebec. However, I don't remember **his / an** name.

2. **Those / This** plan was drawn up by me, with the help of Mr. Blair. **Their / His** nephew, Harold, also pitched in and helped us collect **a / the** relevant data. Mr. Blair then did **a / an** analysis. We are going to present **the / these** plan to **a / those** committee **this / that** Friday so that we can get it rolling early next week.

3. They finally came up with **these / an** alternative – to let Jeff take up **their / those** assignment. Although Jeff was not **a / the** best choice, **the / that** president agreed that he should be able to execute it properly.

4. **A / The** pollution in **these / this** city is worsening at **a / an** alarming rate. We all need to ensure that we do **your / our** part in being responsible citizens. We can start by stopping the use of **this / those** non-recyclable plastic bags, which are littering **a / the** area.

Possessive nouns, quantifiers, and numbers are also used as determiners preceding nouns to modify them.

Examples

- Possessive Noun:
  Mom's dress is pretty.
- Quantifier:
  I have many friends.
- Number:
  One apple is enough.

D. Fill in the blanks with the correct determiners.

Possessive Noun		Quantifier		Number	
house's	Troy's	each	not many	one	three

1. ______________ people understand the rules of the game.

2. ______________ thing is for sure: I will not give in no matter what happens.

3. ______________ intelligence got him out of many difficult situations.

4. The ______________ rent will go up next year.

5. ______________ detail of his new plan was perfectly executed.

6. ______________ paintings out of four were sold at the auction.

My Notes

____

____

____

____

UNIT 2

Perfect Tenses

The **present perfect tense** is used for recent actions that affect the present. It is also used for actions that happened at an unspecified time before now.

Present Perfect Tense Form:
has/have (not) + past participle of a verb

Examples

- He has bought a new movie.
- Claudia has seen that movie three times.

A. Fill in the blanks with the present perfect tense of the verbs in parentheses to complete the sentences.

1. He ________________ (watch) five movies since yesterday.
2. I ________________ (not sleep) today.
3. My classes ________________ (not start) this week.
4. Ed ________________ (break) his ankle and has to stay home from school.
5. They ________________ (not meet) for years.
6. The children ________________ (not pack) their bags yet.
7. Their parents ________________ (travel) to many countries.
8. The victim ________________ (accuse) his neighbour of the burglary.
9. The scientists ________________ (write) a report on space invasions.
10. Marlon ________________ (not speak) a word since his dog died.
11. The candle wax ________________ (melt) onto the wooden table.
12. The burden ________________ (fall) on her shoulders now.
13. Tim ________________ (not play) basketball since last week.
14. She ________________ (live) in downtown Toronto since she was a little girl.

The **past perfect tense** is used to indicate that something happened before another action in the past and that an action had been completed before a specific time in the past.

Past Perfect Tense Form:

had (not/never) + past participle of a verb

Examples

- After the children had finished dinner, they helped wash the dishes.
- Before I could catch her, she had grabbed the cookies and disappeared!

B. Put the verbs in the past perfect tense in parentheses.

1. The race had started by the time Jim arrived.
2. We had not met each other before we joined the team in 2017.
3. We had finished painting when he offered to help.
4. Before the police arrested him, they had interviewed many witnesses.
5. My mom had cooked dinner before the guests arrived.
6. They were excited because they had never seen an elephant before.

C. Underline the first event in red and the second event in blue.

It does not matter which event is mentioned first; the past perfect tense makes it clear which happened first.

1. They had a snowball fight after it had snowed earlier that morning.
2. The little girl felt bad as she had broken the vase.
3. Laura did not make it to the finals because she had not practised enough.
4. He had mastered the English language before he came to Canada.
5. She had woken up late so she did not get to school on time.

Section 2 Grammar

The **future perfect tense** is used to show that something will occur before another action in the future, and that something will happen before a specific time in the future.

Future Perfect Tense Form:

will (not) have + past participle of a verb

Examples

- They will have bought a new house by the time the baby arrives.
- By June next year, Jason will have completed his undergraduate studies.

D. Rewrite the sentences in the future perfect tense.

1. In two weeks, I will learn how to play this tune.

____

____

2. Before he leaves, they will get everything ready.

____

3. Lillian will arrive in Italy by the time we get there.

____

4. In less than six months, his brother will achieve his goal.

____

5. Mr. Silver will leave the office by the time we reach him.

____

6. They will master the skill once they complete the training.

____

7. We will reach our destination before sunset.

____

E. **Identify and write the tenses of the sentences in the boxes. Then write sentences of your own with the verbs in the correct tenses.**

1. **Tense**

- be: I have never been to a concert before.
- see: ______________________________

____
- buy: ______________________________

2. **Tense**

- mow: Kurt will have mowed the lawn by tomorrow afternoon.
- do: ______________________________
- paint: ______________________________

3. **Tense**

- arrive: Dad had arrived home before it started snowing.
- think: ______________________________
- choose: ______________________________

My Notes

____

____

____

____

UNIT 3 Noun Phrases

A phrase is a group of words that functions as one unit in a sentence. Each phrase has a word that links it to the rest of the sentence. That word is often referred to as the "head".

A **noun phrase** has a noun as its head. It includes a noun and its modifiers.

Example

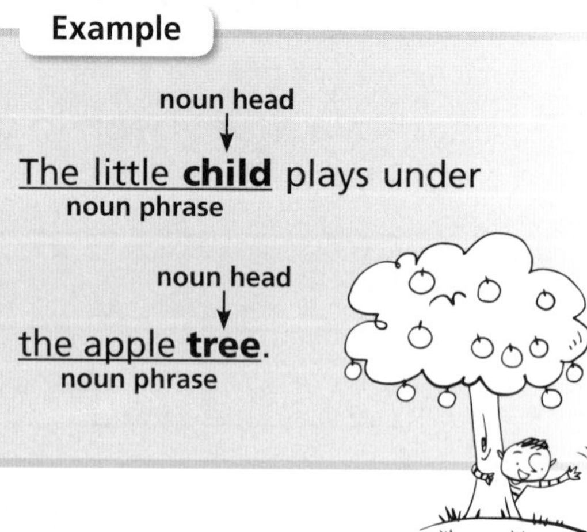

noun head
The little **child** plays under
noun phrase
noun head
the apple **tree**.
noun phrase

A. Underline the noun phrases in the sentences.

1. They did not see the dark tunnel until they almost hit it.
2. For my birthday, she gave me a heart-shaped box.
3. My cousin's neighbour fixed the collapsed fence for him.
4. They were involved in a serious car accident.
5. Look at the little puppy on the rug. Isn't it cute?
6. He crawled through the dark and stuffy attic to find his old comics.
7. There is a shortage of food after the severe flood.
8. The scorching sun made Kevin dizzy and tired.
9. Should we skate over the frozen river?
10. The red brick house is for sale.
11. She baked a bunch of delicious cookies for her daughter's friends.
12. The tourists took a quick detour on their way to Toronto.
13. Her vivid dreams always give her ideas for her beautiful paintings.

B. Underline each noun phrase and circle its head.

1. Dr. Wu appreciated my hard work and determination.
2. I enjoyed watching the spring rain by the open window.
3. Grandma was upset because she lost her walking stick.
4. Julie said, "I cannot eat the burned toast."
5. The fluffy dog barked near the fallen nest.
6. Mrs. Fields is our favourite Math teacher.
7. We have a strong and beautiful relationship.

C. Complete the sentences with noun phrases.

1. Neal reminds me of ________________________.
2. She could not listen to ________________________.
3. He probably completed ________________________.
4. Nobody seems to know ________________________.
5. Leticia deeply cared about ________________________.
6. Has anyone seen ________________________?
7. Once upon a time, there was ________________________.
8. Have you visited ________________________?
9. I would like to watch ________________________.
10. Adam could not eat ________________________.

A noun phrase can function as a subject, a direct object, an indirect object, or the object of a preposition in a sentence.

Example

The vet (subject) fed Doug the Dog (indirect object) some pet food (direct object) at the shelter (object of a preposition).

D. Identify the functions of the underlined noun phrases in the sentences. Write "S" for subjects, "DO" for direct objects, "IO" for indirect objects, and "OP" for objects of prepositions.

1. The beautiful garden featured a hand-crafted water fountain. ____
2. Judy was able to score the winning goal for her team! ____
3. The public did not believe her implausible story. ____
4. The poor cat was stuck on the steep roof for hours. ____
5. The babysitter read the sleepy boy a story. ____
6. Gary wandered among the tall trees before finding his way back home. ____
7. The teacher mailed the principal an acceptance letter. ____
8. Myrtle could not save her mother's favourite vase from shattering to pieces. ____
9. No one in the courtroom was ready for the verdict to be read. ____
10. Her only hope was gone when the fire burned out. ____
11. The flight attendant greeted the passengers on the plane. ____
12. Dad built Lily an intricate sandcastle. ____

E. **Put the words in order to form a noun phrase and write it in the box. Then make a sentence using the noun phrase with the function indicated.**

1. **direct object**

   glass milk a of

2. **subject**

   house over the haunted there

3. **object of a preposition**

   new her laptop

4. **indirect object**

   baby crying the

5. **object of a preposition**

   the cake baked freshly

My Notes

Section 2 Grammar

UNIT 4 Adjective and Adjectival Phrases

An **adjective phrase** has an adjective as its head and functions as an adjective.

An **adjectival phrase** can be any phrase that functions like an adjective and does not need an adjective as its head. It is usually hyphenated.

Examples

- It was <u>awfully silly</u> (adjective phrase) of you to wear this hat.
- It was a <u>two-hour</u> (adjectival phrase) drive to the farm.

A. Check to show whether the underlined phrases in the sentences are adjective phrases or adjectival phrases.

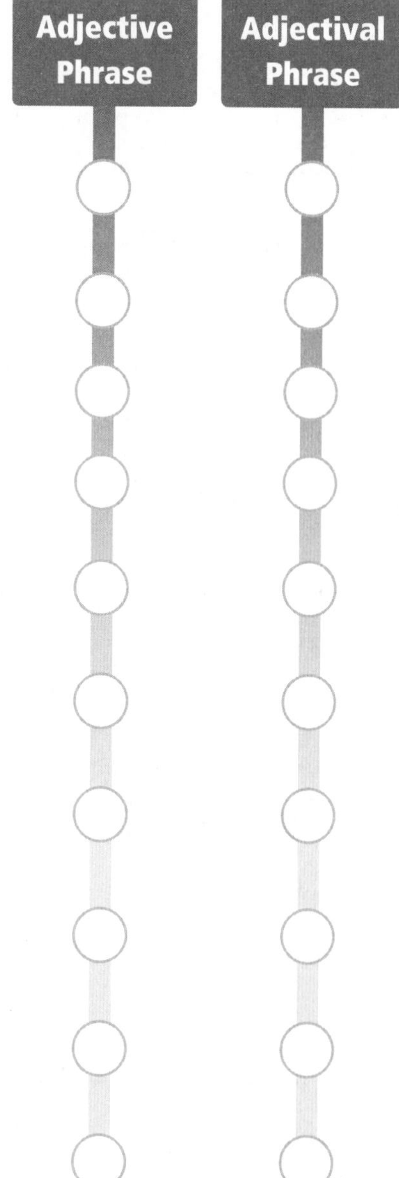

	Adjective Phrase	Adjectival Phrase
1. I'm sure you can do an <u>even better</u> job next time.	◯	◯
2. They will conduct an <u>in-depth</u> investigation into the burglary.	◯	◯
3. All of us are receiving <u>on-the-job</u> training.	◯	◯
4. Can a <u>six-year-old</u> boy see this new action movie?	◯	◯
5. Wait until the T-shirt is <u>completely dry</u> before wearing it.	◯	◯
6. They made a <u>last-minute</u> decision to host the dinner.	◯	◯
7. The children were <u>awfully sad</u> when they had to leave.	◯	◯
8. My friends ordered an <u>excessively large</u> pizza on Friday.	◯	◯
9. The students were annoyed by her <u>know-it-all</u> attitude.	◯	◯
10. Did you know that the <u>very kind</u> shopkeeper gave me a discount?	◯	◯

B. Circle the adjective phrase in each sentence. Then draw an arrow to show the noun or pronoun that it modifies.

An adjective phrase functions like an adjective to modify a noun or a pronoun in a sentence.

a (big fluffy) dog

1. The wind blew her wavy brown hair when she ran.
2. His new white shirt had stains on it.
3. He was very surprised to find a chipmunk in the attic.
4. I have never met an artist more talented than him.
5. They are truly sorry about what they have done.
6. I am quite serious about what I just suggested.
7. The weather was not too bad when we walked our dog.
8. Isabelle is reading a particularly interesting fantasy story.

Section 2 Grammar

C. Fill in the blanks with the correct adjectival phrases to complete the sentences.

Adjectival Phrases

state-of-the-art
well-kept
up-to-date
last-minute
end-of-season

1. We need ________________ information on global warming.
2. The Fashion Factory's ________________ sale starts tomorrow!
3. Our flight experienced a ________________ delay because of the snowstorm.
4. This is truly a ________________ home theatre!
5. The famous chef's cheesecake recipe is a ________________ secret.

D. Identify and write the underlined phrases in the correct boxes.

Anna did not like the <u>newly released</u> movie she was watching with her friends at the theatre, so she decided to wander around while it was playing.

She aimlessly followed the <u>glow-in-the-dark</u> signs on the floor and came to an <u>extremely dark</u> room. As her eyes adjusted, she felt as if she had been there before. Then she spotted a <u>self-help</u> book on the desk. It was written by Professor Mackenzie – that was her father's name!

The <u>easy-to-remember</u> title and the image of an <u>unusually strange</u> man on the cover took Anna to her earliest memory: her <u>then-thirty-year-old</u> father reading a book in a rocking chair. She was deeply lost in her thoughts when she heard the commotion outside.

The movie had just ended and the <u>brightly-lit</u> hallway was now full of <u>extremely excited</u> movie goers. As she closed the door of the dark room behind her, she smiled and exited the theatre with its <u>up-to-date</u> posters of movies and the <u>very comforting</u> image of her father's book.

Maybe this place had once been the library Dad used to take me to, she silently concluded to herself.

Adjective Phrase	Adjectival Phrase

E. **Circle the adjective and adjectival phrases in the sentences and circle to tell the types of phrases they are. Then use each phrase to form a sentence of your own.**

Phrase

1. The small colourful figurine adorned the coffee table. **Adjective / Adjectival**

   My Sentence ____________________

2. Karen's on-the-go outfit was worn out. **Adjective / Adjectival**

   My Sentence ____________________

3. The highly motivated actor will achieve great success. **Adjective / Adjectival**

   My Sentence ____________________

4. Matt's do-it-yourself attitude is a sign of independence. **Adjective / Adjectival**

   My Sentence ____________________

5. This is an easy-to-remember recipe. **Adjective / Adjectival**

   My Sentence ____________________

My Notes

UNIT 5 Prepositional Phrases

A **prepositional phrase** consists of a preposition and its object. The preposition is the head of the phrase. The object of the preposition can be a noun, pronoun, or gerund, or noun clause. The object can also have modifiers.

Examples

- She is at home.
  (at – preposition; home – noun)
- They stopped her from excessive eating.
  (from – preposition; excessive – modifier; eating – gerund)

A. Underline the prepositional phrases in the sentences.

1. He cautiously walked around it.
2. I saw a beautiful mermaid by the light of the moon.
3. Stan talked extensively about how he lost weight.
4. My sister wished me good luck wholeheartedly before leaving.
5. She realized that another woman was standing in front of her.
6. My favourite movie is playing at the nearest theatre.
7. Mom sewed a cute ladybug on my new dress.
8. The environmentalist lectured against littering.
9. The white coat in my mother's hallway closet was made in Sweden.
10. Can you please tell me the story after school?
11. Please put the most delicate vase on the highest shelf.
12. They sat by the campfire singing songs all night long.

B. Circle to identify the head of each prepositional phrase for each sentence.

1. Walking through the thick forest is not a good idea.
2. After him, she was our best bet.
3. Dani always wanted to go beyond the boundary.

4. The car struck a tree after it went off the road.

5. Being with family and friends is what makes the holiday season special.
6. She supported her brother in whatever he did.
7. Dr. Salma said, "Your headaches could be the result of constant worrying."

C. Complete the table by writing the parts of the prepositional phrases in the sentences.

1. The painting with the green balloons is my mother's.
2. We have snacks for when we get hungry.
3. Don't worry! I believe our team can still win without me.
4. After a delicious dinner, the family sat together and watched a movie.
5. Before strenuous exercise, drinking water is important.

	Preposition +	Modifier(s) +	Noun/Pronoun/Gerund/Clause
1.			
2.			
3.			
4.			
5.			

A prepositional phrase can function as an adjective or an adverb in a sentence. As an adjective, it answers the question "Which?" and as an adverb, it answers the question "How?", "When?", or "Where?".

D. Circle ADJ for adjective or ADV for adverb to show whether the underlined prepositional phrase in each sentence is functioning as an adjective or an adverb.

1. The lamp on the coffee table is broken. **ADJ / ADV**
2. I am impressed with how you executed the plan. **ADJ / ADV**
3. The man in the clearing scared Julian and his friends. **ADJ / ADV**
4. The candles were kept under the sink. **ADJ / ADV**
5. The money on the dresser is mine. **ADJ / ADV**
6. The letter from Stacey could not be found. **ADJ / ADV**
7. This colour looks really good on you. **ADJ / ADV**
8. Everybody got sick after eating. **ADJ / ADV**
9. For her, the rain was a blessing. **ADJ / ADV**
10. The boy who got up without crying is exceptionally resilient! **ADJ / ADV**
11. The paramedic held her hand to stop her from scratching. **ADJ / ADV**
12. The puppy in the playpen jumped up and down. **ADJ / ADV**
13. They laughed as the birds flew over them. **ADJ / ADV**

E. Complete the sentences with prepositional phrases. Then circle to tell whether they function as adjectives (ADJ) or adverbs (ADV). Use as many different prepositions as possible.

A prepositional phrase never contains the subject of a sentence.

1. There was a pile of clothes and I stepped ________________ **ADJ / ADV** .
2. Her father gave her a brand new phone ________________ **ADJ / ADV** .
3. The kite flew ________________ **ADJ / ADV** .
4. All the students are playing ________________ **ADJ / ADV** .
5. Anthony wrote a book ________________ **ADJ / ADV** .
6. ________________ **ADJ / ADV** , dinosaurs roamed the Earth.
7. He closed his eyes ________________ **ADJ / ADV** .
8. ________________ **ADJ / ADV** , she took a deep breath.
9. You are the best father ________________ **ADJ / ADV** .
10. She ran ________________ **ADJ / ADV** to catch the bus.
11. The farmer is tired ________________ **ADJ / ADV** .
12. Susie was careless and tripped ________________ **ADJ / ADV** .

My Notes

UNIT 6

Noun and Adverb Clauses

A **clause** has the same structure as a sentence but it is part of a larger sentence.

A **noun clause** is a dependent clause that functions as a noun in a sentence. It can act as a subject, a direct or indirect object, an object of a preposition, or a subject complement.

Examples

- Whoever finds it will be rewarded. (subject)
- The boy confessed that he had stolen the pencil. (direct object)
- The host gave whoever came to the event a gift. (indirect object)
- Vote for whomever you want. (object of a preposition)
- His biggest regret was that he gave up. (subject complement)

A. Check if the underlined clauses are noun clauses.

Noun Clause

1. Who speaks first does not matter that much. ☐
2. Let me know what you think about the proposal. ☐
3. He was asked to say whatever was on his mind. ☐
4. Whoever has the access card can enter the office. ☐
5. I do not understand why she said that. ☐
6. I know why he did not laugh. ☐
7. This bench is where we used to sit. ☐
8. What he said inspired everyone in the audience. ☐
9. I understand that he will not be able to make it today. ☐
10. It is a mystery that he came back. ☐
11. You should be kind to whomever you meet. ☐
12. I don't know whether it will rain today. ☐

B. Identify the functions of the underlined noun clauses and write the sentence numbers in the correct boxes.

1. That he had even implied it made her suspicious.
2. The grumpy old man gives whoever walks across his yard a lecture!
3. The problem was that she did not know how to drive.
4. Lordana thought about what her mother had told her.
5. They all knew why he was not participating in the race.
6. What the CEO said in his speech troubled the company.
7. Claudia was focused on when the bell would ring.
8. I do not think what Mr. Clyde said makes sense.
9. You are responsible for whatever you do.
10. Whether you will be admitted to the university is uncertain.
11. Michael's mistake is that he did not practise.
12. Always write whoever writes you a letter back.

Sentences with Noun Clauses Functioning as:

Subject	Direct Object	Indirect Object	Object of a Preposition	Subject Complement

Section 2 Grammar

An **adverb clause** is a dependent clause that functions as an adverb in a sentence. There are adverb clauses of place, time, reason, purpose, contrast, and condition.

Examples

- <u>Unless it rains</u>, we will stick to our plan.
  condition
- You must not use your phone <u>while you are driving</u>.
  time

C. **Underline the adverb clauses in the sentences.**

1. If we do not hurry, we will be late for the train.
2. The ceremony will begin once the guest of honour arrives.
3. The teacher repeated the lesson because Aiden did not understand it.
4. The little children had to stay in the playroom until their mothers came to pick them up.
5. They ate and ate as if they had been starving for weeks!
6. The guests arrived while you were sleeping.
7. I miss you whenever I drive across the street you lived on.
8. After they had finished breakfast, his cousins went out to play.
9. Although he studied a lot, he panicked during the exam.
10. Since I am working tonight, I will see the movie tomorrow.
11. I will stay in touch with you wherever you are.
12. Nobody will know unless you tell them.
13. Cecil will not give up even if he fails again.
14. I could not play the game because I hurt my foot.

D. Put the adverb clauses in parentheses. Then write the sentence numbers in the correct boxes.

1. He came early so that he could have some time to rehearse.
2. Before the coach arrived, they were just sitting there chatting.
3. Mrs. Winter was upset because Matt and Joe misbehaved in class.
4. If you listen to me, you will not get yourself into trouble.
5. Wherever he goes, he brings along his lucky charm – a gold coin his grandpa has given him.
6. Cassie made detailed notes so that she could remember everything for her test.
7. All the birds scattered once they saw the scarecrow.
8. Although we seldom see each other now, we remain best friends.
9. Since Peter had never skied before, he was a bit nervous.

Adverb Clause of					
Place	Time	Reason	Purpose	Contrast	Condition

My Notes

Section 2 Grammar

UNIT 7

Relative Clauses

A **relative clause** is a subordinate clause that helps identify someone or something by providing information about it.

It is also called an adjectival clause since it identifies or describes a noun, like an adjective does.

Example

I want to live in a castle where there are lots of candies!
relative clause

A. Put parentheses around the relative clauses in the sentences.

1. The actor who played the king was very convincing.
2. The socks that I bought last month are already torn!
3. The poet, whose name was Edgar, wrote well into the night.
4. My father, who is a scientist, knows a lot about robots.
5. The crop that we harvested this year was plentiful!
6. The student whose desk is at the back of the class is brilliant.
7. Katie Joan, who received this year's award, was the only actress in the movie.
8. 2015 was the year when my family came to live in Canada.
9. Parliament Hill, which is in Ottawa, is a majestic place.
10. Toronto is the city where I was born.
11. The man, whose son is my neighbour, is in the hospital.
12. This is the bike that I have wanted for years!

A relative clause:

- comes immediately after the noun it relates to.
- begins with a relative pronoun: who, whom, which, whose, or that; or a relative adverb: where, when, or why.

Examples

- **Mr. Khan**, whom you admire, is lecturing at the university this summer. (**Mr. Khan**: noun)
- The **pencil** that you gave me was broken. (**pencil**: noun)
- The **reason** why you left early was not a good one. (**reason**: noun)

B. Circle the correct relative pronouns or relative adverbs for the sentences.

1. The player was using a bat **that / who** was too long for him.
2. That is the building **where / that** Jeff works.
3. The tie **whose / that** Paul was wearing tonight belongs to me.
4. Dr. Martin, **when / who** turned 50 last week, has been our family doctor for ten years.
5. The video game **whose / which** was released yesterday is sold out.

6. Mrs. Walsh, **whom / that** everybody likes, is leaving the school in June.
7. This is the restaurant **when / where** I got my first job.
8. My yacht, **whose / which** I bought last year, has a blue mast.
9. Is this the new dress **where / that** you mentioned?
10. When we are asleep, our dreams take us to imaginary places **where / which** anything can happen.
11. Tell me the reason **where / why** you did not share the pizza!
12. The day **where / when** we met was a beautiful sunny day.
13. I love the book **that / who** my dad wrote!
14. Do you know the girl **whose / whom** mother works here?

There are two types of relative clauses.

Defining Relative Clause:
identifies or describes a particular person or thing

Non-defining Relative Clause:
provides additional information about a person or thing; separated from the main sentence by commas

Examples

- Defining Relative Clause:
  Did you meet the player who scored the last goal?
- Non-defining Relative Clause:
  Beatrice, who scored the last goal, was the best on her team.

C. Underline the relative clauses and identify them as defining or non-defining. Write the sentence numbers on the lines.

1. Mrs. Green, who taught us History last year, will retire this summer.
2. The teacher who taught us History last year will retire this summer.
3. Yesterday on my way home, I met a man who asked me about Tim.
4. Yesterday on my way home, I met Mr. Jenkins, who asked me about Tim.
5. My brother broke the watch that I had given him for his birthday.
6. My brother broke his watch, which I had given him for his birthday.
7. We all enjoyed the story, which ended on a happy note.
8. I find the story that Bill told me hard to believe.
9. She is the dancer who mesmerized the audience with her spectacular performance.
10. The dancer, who mesmerized the audience with her spectacular performance, will leave the troupe soon.

Defining Relative Clause: ______________________

Non-defining Relative Clause: ______________________

D. Complete the sentences with the specified relative clauses.

Defining Relative Clause

1. A cat ______________________________

____

2. If you happen to come across a man ______________________________

____

3. This morning, I saw a car ______________________________

____

Non-defining Relative Clause

1. I spoke to the school librarian, ______________________________

____

2. Sitting over there is Mr. Johnson, ______________________________

____

3. Jasmine and Derek played in the backyard, ______________________________

____

4. Georgia saves a toonie in her piggy bank, ______________________________

____

My Notes

____

____

____

____

UNIT 8 Modifiers

A **modifier** adds information to another element in a sentence. It can be an adjective or an adverb, or it can be a phrase or a clause functioning as an adjective or an adverb.

Examples

- She felt awkward (adjective) to approach him for help.
- The plan should have been executed more carefully (adverb phrase).
- The man who saved the cat (adjectival clause) is my neighbour.

A. Identify the underlined modifiers and write the sentence numbers in the correct places.

1. Do you remember the restaurant where we tried the best ever soufflé?
2. Could you tell me the title of the book that you mentioned last night again?
3. They are working hard to make sure that they can meet the deadline.
4. In order not to be discovered, he snuck into the room very quietly.
5. He did it so badly that he dared not submit it to the committee.
6. Jimmy and his family flew back home when the trip was over.
7. Mr. Flores locked the exceptionally rare gemstone in his safe.
8. The attack was simply a cowardly act.
9. Sofia pretended that she did not know the truth.
10. I can see the moon in the clear, dark blue night sky.

Adjective: ______________________

Adjective Phrase: ______________________

Adjectival Clause: ______________________

Adverb: ______________________

Adverb Phrase: ______________________

Adverbial Clause: ______________________

The modifiers "**good**" and "**bad**" are adjectives, whereas "**well**" and "**badly**" are adverbs.

Examples

Adjective:

- This story is a good read.
- Gina has a bad memory.

Adverb:

- My mom dances well.
- I always draw badly.

B. Circle the correct modifiers to complete the sentences.

1. Katie thought that the singing competition was a **good / well** opportunity for her. If she did **well / bad**, she would stand a chance to be one of the finalists. Last time, she did so **bad / badly** that she was eliminated in the first round.

2. We consider it a **good / bad** idea because we will not be able to get any support. We should think **good / well** and come up with a strategy that is **good / well** enough to win at least four votes. We should not do too **bad / badly** then.

C. Check the circles if the modifiers in the sentences are correct. If not, cross out the wrong modifiers and write the correct ones above them.

1. Nelly plays the piano well and she feels good about it. ◯
2. James does not play the piano good but he is pretty well with the cello. ◯
3. Mr. Wilkinson does not seem to feel good today; he looks really pale. ◯
4. The trip was bad planned so everyone was upset. ◯
5. Liana admitted that she had made a badly mistake. ◯
6. He felt bad for causing us so much trouble. ◯

A **dangling modifier** refers to a modifier that modifies something that it should not. When constructing a sentence, we should keep the modifier close to the words that it modifies to avoid confusion in the meaning.

Examples

- Walking down the street, the morning air refreshed me. (✗)
- Walking down the street, I found the morning air refreshing. (✓)

D. Read each sentence and decide if there is any dangling modifier. If there is, rewrite the sentence in the correct way.

1. Having finished cleaning, the music was turned on.

   ____

2. To improve his results, he conducted the survey again.

   ____

3. After reviewing her thesis, the argument remained inconclusive.

   ____

4. Hoping to be excused, the doctor's note was given to the manager.

   ____

5. Before leaving for work, my cat played with me for a while.

   ____

6. Without anything better to do, going shopping would be good for us.

   ____

   ____

7. To train a dog to be obedient, you need to be patient.

   ____

   ____

E. **Rewrite and complete the story using as many modifiers as possible to make it interesting.**

Remember to put the modifiers close to the words they modify.

Arnold felt movement inside the house. He walked around to see what was going on. He heard noises. Before he could see anything, Arnold found himself on the ground...

____

____

____

____

____

____

____

____

____

____

____

My Notes

____

____

____

____

UNIT 9 Transition Words and Phrases

Transition words and **phrases** are used to connect ideas and sentences. They help make a text sound smooth and more coherent.

There are different types of transition words and phrases. They are used to show addition, contrast, examples, comparison, and much more.

Examples

- I am exhausted. In other words, I need a break!
- Alina loves to make mosaics. Similarly, Samuel does too.

A. Put the transition words and phrases in the sentences in parentheses.

1. Ayan does not have a healthful diet. For example, he always eats ice cream with fries for breakfast.
2. Shiela did not fix the roof properly. Nonetheless, the owner ignored her mistakes.
3. Human beings feel pain when they get injured. In the same way, animals feel pain when we hurt them.
4. Ella never wanted to play with kids her own age. On the other hand, she liked spending time with her seven-year-old best friend, Katie.
5. I like to swim on the weekends. In fact, it is my favourite activity.
6. He did not wash all the dishes. However, his mother still allowed him to play.
7. Plants make food through the process of photosynthesis. In other words, plants need the energy of the sun to survive.
8. My teacher thought I had understood today's lecture. On the contrary, I could not even hear half of it because of the construction noise outside.
9. We need to preserve our natural resources. Moreover, we should be aware of the long-term effects of climate change.
10. The parts of this machine have been manufactured in different countries. For instance, its battery was imported from Japan.

B. Write the sentence numbers in the correct categories to show what purpose the transition words and phrases serve in the sentences.

1. Jerry made a face when he was presented with broccoli for dinner. Likewise, his twin brother did the same.

2. Mrs. Sanders is benevolent. For instance, she regularly donates to charity.

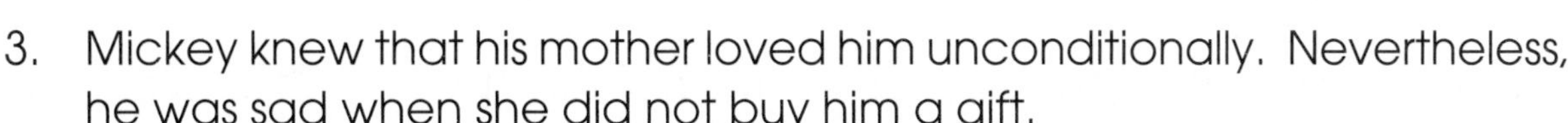

3. Mickey knew that his mother loved him unconditionally. Nevertheless, he was sad when she did not buy him a gift.

4. You can start doing good deeds for others. For example, you can help your father mow the lawn.

5. I do not like the style of this dress. Besides, it is too expensive.

6. Many oil tankers spill oil accidentally. As a result, the aquatic life in the area suffers.

7. She does not read well. Therefore, she is shy whenever the teacher asks her to read to the class.

8. This cheesecake is delicious. Indeed, it is the best cheesecake I have ever had!

9. I have decided to stop eating meat. In fact, I have been careful about my diet for two months now.

10. Bring water with you when you go hiking. Also, do not forget to put on sunscreen.

11. Winter in Canada can be harsh. However, the summer season in most areas is moderate and is welcomed by everyone.

12. I was not affected by her speech. Similarly, most of the judges seemed unmoved as well.

Purpose the Transition Words and Phrases Serve

Contrast: ____________ Addition: ____________ Comparison: ____________

Example: ____________ Emphasis: ____________ Conclusion: ____________

C. Fill in the blanks with the correct transition words and phrases.

Transition Words and Phrases

for that reason **in conclusion**
to repeat **despite that** **also** **eventually**

1. It was raining on Thursday. ______________________, we walked to the convenience store to buy some ice cream.

2. Sarah had been throwing a tantrum while her mother was busy. ______________________, the toddler got tired and fell asleep.

3. Animal testing is a waste of time and money. ______________________, it should be banned altogether.

4. The construction site is dangerous. ______________________, do not go near the area!

5. Harry likes cooking for his family. ______________________, he is a great son.

6. Ida wants to win the figure skating championship. ______________________, she practises every day after school.

D. Write a sentence with a transition word or phrase for each situation.

1. Ali told his father he had won. ______________________
____

2. Dayna is playing for her school's soccer team. ____________
____

3. To bake a delicious cake, make sure you have a good recipe. ____________
____

4. I like going camping with my family. ______________________
____

5. I realized that it was too late to go to the movies. ______________________
____

E. Rewrite the sentences by adding appropriate transition words and phrases. Make any other necessary changes.

1. Sofia was worried about her son's behaviour at school. She was worried about his grades.

2. Kiera loved vegetables. She loved broccoli.

3. Nova was not feeling well on Thursday. She had to call in sick.

4. This sketch is very detailed. That sketch is kind of vague.

5. Julian was an ambitious athlete. He was a great student.

6. The service was extremely poor. We had a great time.

My Notes

UNIT 10 Introductory Words, Phrases, and Clauses

Introductory words go at the beginning of a sentence. They are set off from the main clause by a comma. Most introductory words are adverbs and are also used as transition words. Interjections are also used as introductory words.

Examples

- Suddenly, she started choking.
  adverb
- Yes, your house is beautiful.
  interjection

A. Fill in the blanks with the correct introductory words.

Introductory Words

please **no** **fortunately** **sorry** **ugh** **meanwhile**
sadly **yes** **suddenly** **definitely** **finally**

1. ______________, may I have some more pizza?
2. ______________, we will look into the matter.
3. ______________, there is a fly in my soup!
4. ______________, the genie appeared out of thin air!
5. ______________, she was waiting for her son at the airport.
6. ______________, Charles, but I would never betray my friend.
7. ______________, I cannot help you with your homework.
8. ______________, you look amazing in that dress.

9. ______________, we could not complete the quest soon enough.
10. ______________, the runner has reached the finish line.
11. ______________, she has some savings. That is why she is not worried.

An **introductory phrase** is a phrase that introduces the main clause in a sentence. It does not have its own subject and verb.

Types of introductory phrases include: prepositional phrases, appositive phrases, participial phrases, and infinitive phrases.

Introductory phrases are set off by a comma.

Examples

- <u>Before the ceremony</u>, she lost her tiara.
  prepositional phrase
- <u>An amazing soccer player</u>, Lionel Messi has a lot of fans.
  appositive phrase
- <u>Picking up her keys</u>, she ran out the door.
  participial phrase
- <u>To hide her secrets</u>, she put her diary in the pillow.
  infinitive phrase

Section 2

Grammar

B. Underline the introductory phrase in each sentence. Then write to tell what type of introductory phrase it is.

Types of Introductory Phrases

prepositional
appositive
participial
infinitive

1. An experienced art teacher, Mr. Sanders is very talented. ____________
2. After the storm, the children came out to play. ____________
3. A spoiled child, Sam does not listen to anyone. ____________
4. To reach her office on time, she had to take a cab. ____________
5. Having been a nurse, Jane knew how to remain calm during emergencies. ____________
6. Driving through the green meadows, Irena felt at peace. ____________
7. To guard the barrack, the soldiers took turns in pairs. ____________
8. Before the applause, Jamil had no idea he had been selected. ____________
9. During the ceremony, nobody moved or said a word. ____________
10. To make pickled mangoes, you have to use the right ingredients. ____________

An **introductory clause** is a dependent clause (containing a subject and a verb) that introduces the main clause in a sentence.

Introductory clauses are always set off by a comma.

Examples

- As we drove through the tunnel, a blinding light pierced the darkness.
- If they want to play, they should be on time.

C. Write an introductory clause to complete each sentence.

1. ____,
we decided to go to the beach.

2. ____,
she did not win the first prize.

3. ____,
Dennis noticed a suspicious car in front of his house.

4. ____,
Regina would have to ask for help.

5. ____,
I did not get enough sleep.

6. ____,
Richard was not in the mood for an argument.

7. ________________________________,
they headed out early in the morning.

8. ________________________________,
Elena hid behind the bushes.

9. ________________________________,
the babysitter was exhausted.

10. ________________________________,
a mouse darted out.

D. **Fill in the blanks with the letters of the correct introductory words, phrases, and clauses to complete the story.**

A Startled by the noise	F Feeling relieved
B Frozen in place	G Resolutely
C After a moment	H No matter what
D Feeling a cool breeze	I As she trudged through the grass
E Late Friday evening	J If she thought about the safety of her home

1.______ , Ellie went out into her dark and foggy backyard. The woods behind her house always scared her, and she wanted to prove that she could be brave. 2.______ , she zipped up her jacket. 3.______ , she could conquer her fears. 4.______ , she felt a twig snap under her foot. 5.______ , Ellie had to pause and take a breath. That was when she noticed the eyes – a pair of unblinking eyes watching her from deep within the woods. 6.______ , she felt fear unfurl in her chest. But then she remembered what her mother always told her: it was okay to feel fear; you just had to make sure you pushed past it. 7.______ , she stared right back into those eyes, despite her fear. 8.______ , the eyes blinked and backed away into the woods. 9.______ , Ellie walked back to her house. 10.______ , home was a safe place she never had to be afraid of.

My Notes

____

____

____

____

UNIT 11 Punctuation

We use a **colon** to set off a list, an explanation, or a quotation, much like a pointer telling the reader what is about to follow the main part of the sentence.

Example

Your writing should include these**:** the introduction, the body, and the conclusion.

A. Check the sentence with the colon in the correct place for each pair.

1. (A) Remember: what John F. Kennedy said "We need men who can dream of things that never were."

   (B) Remember what John F. Kennedy said: "We need men who can dream of things that never were."

2. (A) The coach needed two things from us: our desire to win and our faith in him.

   (B) The coach needed two things: from us our desire to win and our faith in him.

3. (A) Do you know who said: this "Truth is what stands the test of experience"?

   (B) Do you know who said this: "Truth is what stands the test of experience"?

4. (A) There remained one problem we had: to win Jerry over.

   (B) There remained one problem: we had to win Jerry over.

5. (A) The zoo has some new animals: two giraffes, two cheetahs, and six penguins.

   (B) The zoo has some new animals two: giraffes, two cheetahs, and six penguins.

We use a **semicolon** to:

- sort out a long list.
- separate closely related independent clauses.

Examples

- There were representatives from Toronto, Ontario**;** Victoria, British Columbia, and Edmonton, Alberta.
- The train arrives at 7:35 a.m. every day**;** it is always on schedule.

B. Put semicolons and colons in the boxes.

1. The batter keyed up ☐ he waited patiently for a pitch.
2. The couple invited several distinguished guests to the reception ☐ Mrs. Weir, Principal of St. Peter's School ☐ Professor Swire, trustee of the University of Toronto ☐ Mr. Sam Watson, MPP Scarborough East, and David Nunn, Executive Director, The Knowledge Bank, Ontario Chapter.
3. There was only one thing remaining on her to-do list ☐ make an appointment with Mr. Cook on or before Tuesday.
4. He did not sleep well ☐ it was too hot and humid.
5. The doctor can tell that there is something wrong with her ☐ she is panting.
6. You need the following to succeed ☐ motivation, commitment, and perseverance.
7. My grandmother used to get up very early ☐ she enjoyed the atmosphere at daybreak.
8. I stuffed my backpack with everything ☐ snacks, utensils, tools, and even shoes!

Parentheses are used to enclose additional information.

Parentheses may be used:

- to add a comment, a date, or a citation to a statement.
- to break the flow of words.
- to show letters and numbers.
- to designate a series of items.
- to provide optional information.

Examples

- I have tried everything **(**well, maybe not everything**)** to lose weight but it has been in vain.
- The University of Toronto **(**U of T**)** has another campus in Scarborough.
- Before swimming, you should **(**1**)** wear goggles, **(**2**)** put on a life jacket, and **(**3**)** ensure there is adult supervision.
- Please RSVP for your child**(**ren**)**.

C. Match each sentence with the purpose of the parentheses. Write the letters.

1. Select the unit(s) you would like to discuss. ____
2. Sir Walter Hopkins (1908 – 1956) founded the Hopkins Foundation. ____
3. Nobody (in his or her right mind) would opt out. ____

Purpose

A to add a date

B to provide options

C to provide additional information

D. Add parentheses where needed.

1. The company offered me a good salary $5000/month.
2. National Aeronautics and Space Administration NASA was founded in 1958.
3. The second book was published in Chicago, Illinois see Footnote 5.
4. I did not realize or maybe I did but I did not want to accept it that it had been my fault all along.
5. Which of the following is correct?

   a The green light signals the cars to stop.

   b The red light signals the cars to stop.

   c The yellow light signals the cars to stop.

Quotation marks are used to:

- quote exact spoken or written words.
- show titles.
- introduce new or unusual words and terms.
- show a different use of a common word or to show sarcasm.
- emphasize a letter, word, or phrase.

Examples

- Direct Quote: "I love you," said Mom.
- Title: "The Sleeping Beauty" was a popular movie.
- New Term: "Going green" is so in!
- Sarcasm: I know you were "studying" with the TV on.
- Emphasis: The meaning of the word "confused" is unclear.

Section 2 Grammar

E. Add quotation marks where needed.

1. What? You didn't tell me you are moving! Abbie yelled.
2. Her Royal Highness is the movie I am going to watch today.
3. Your smile is not fooling anyone because there is sadness in your eyes.
4. The i in the word igloo is not capitalized because it is a common noun.
5. Please open your books to Laws of the Universe on page 51.
6. The Oompa Loompas were Willy Wonka's latest creation.
7. To form the plural, add es after box.
8. Fragile is an adjective, not a verb.

My Notes

A. Circle the answers.

1. The quantifier "not any" is used for ______ .

   countable nouns

   uncountable nouns

   both countable and uncountable nouns

2. Which determiners are correct in the sentence below?

   ______ clock is ______ gift for you.

   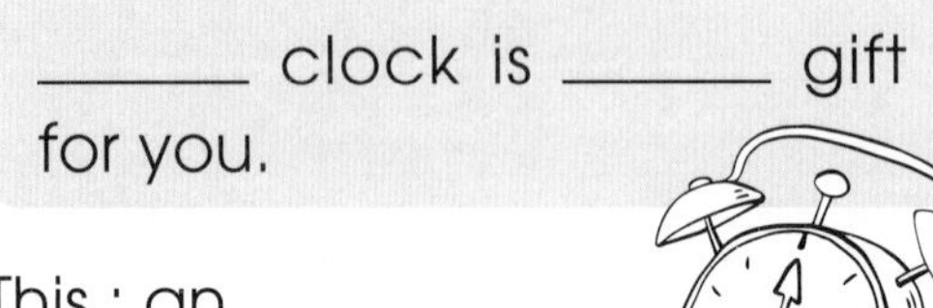

   This ; an

   These ; my

   This ; a

3. What is the verb tense in the sentence below?

   Sarah has not written a single word!

   present perfect tense

   past perfect tense

   future perfect tense

4. How is the future perfect tense formed?

   had (not/never) + past participle of a verb

   will (not) have + past participle of a verb

   has/have (not) + past participle of a verb

5. A noun phrase cannot function as ______ in a sentence.

   a direct object

   an object of a preposition

   an adverb clause

6. Which sentence contains an adjectival phrase?

   It was a hundred-year-old castle.

   It was an extremely old castle.

   It was a historic castle.

7. Which phrase is usually hyphenated?

   an adjective phrase

   an adjectival phrase

   an adverb phrase

8. What does the prepositional phrase function as in the sentence below?

   The eggs in the basket are boiled.

   a noun

   an adjective

   an adverb

9. Which sentence has the noun clause underlined?

   You can have whatever you want.

   You can have the apples only.

   You cannot have anything.

10. What is the underlined adverb clause in the sentence below?

    If I win, I will get a cookie.

    adverb clause of place

    adverb clause of time

    adverb clause of condition

11. A relative clause is also called an adjectival clause because it identifies or describes ______ .

    an adjective

    a noun

    a verb

12. Which relative pronoun is correct in the relative clause below?

    The mat ______ I bought was torn.

    who

    where

    that

13. ______ can be used as introductory words.

    Noun phrases

    Conjunctions

    Interjections

14. Which transition word is correct in the sentence below?

    Joy loves to laugh. ______ , she is sad today.

    However

    Similarly

    Therefore

15. A semicolon cannot be used to ______ .

    sort out a long list

    set off direct quotes

    separate closely related independent clauses

16. ______ are used to enclose additional information.

    Colons

    Quotation marks

    Parentheses

Quantifiers and Perfect Tenses

B. Underline each quantifier. Then write "CN" if it modifies a countable noun and "UN" if it modifies an uncountable noun above it.

Jade stomped into her room after spending several hours justifying her obsession with eating a lot of sugary sweets to her mother. *Why can't Mom just allow me a bit of freedom?* she mulled as she got ready for bed.

The problem was that Jade's mother was a dentist who knew the numerous effects of tooth decay. She only allowed Jade to have a few candies a week. However, Jade loved everything sweet! Also, her mother made her brush and floss regularly and Jade hated both activities! Furthermore, Jade had convinced herself that the cavities, bacteria, and plaque her mother kept talking about were not real.

Therefore, frustrated and angry, Jade went to bed. At least she had her dreams to give her some peace and happiness.

C. Rewrite each sentence to change the tense to the specified tense.

1. After she drifted off to sleep, Jade had a very strange dream.

   Past Perfect Tense:

   ____

2. Jade was walking into a forest full of sugary sweets in her dream.

   Present Perfect Tense:

   ____

   ____

Noun, Adjective, Adjectival, and Prepositional Phrases

D. Write the numbers to sort the phrases into the correct categories.

1 The hungry girl made sure she tasted the **2** deliciously sweet treats along the **3** five-minute walk to a clearing. She came **4** to a curiously strange little town. To her surprise, it was populated with **5** many tiny gingerbread people!

Jade sat down by a **6** fast flowing river of maple syrup and discreetly watched them going about their day. They did everything so merrily – **7** from baking, **8** to singing, **9** to busily collecting **10** the massive amount of honey that seemed to flow out of the **11** state-of-the-art fountains built everywhere in **12** the small town. Jade smiled as **13** a group of gingerbread women gave **14** their hungry children **15** some ice cream.

Overwhelmed and grinning **16** from ear to ear, Jade made a **17** spur-of-the-moment decision: she was going to gobble up all of the mouthwatering sweets **18** in front of her!

As her mother was not there to stop her **19** from excessive eating, that was exactly what she did next!

1. Noun Phrase Functioning as the

   Subject: ____________________

   Direct Object: ____________________

   Indirect Object: ____________________

   Object of a Preposition:

   ____

2. Prepositional Phrase Functioning as an

   Adjective: ____________________

   Adverb: ____________________

3. Adjective Phrase:

   ____

   Adjectival Phrase:

   ____

Noun, Adverb, and Relative Clauses

E. Underline and identify the noun, adverb, and relative clauses.

Type of Clause

1. Jade chomped and chewed on the sugary sweets as if she had never eaten anything before!

2. She ate whatever she could get her hands on – candies, cakes, pies, – and even slurped the chocolate from the chocolate fountains.

3. Jade did not pay attention to the gingerbread people because she was so busy feasting.

4. She did not care about what would happen to the little town she was destroying.

5. In her greed, she threw whatever she could not finish to the side in a pile.

6. The townspeople gathered around Jade in shock while she ruined their beautiful land.

7. They climbed onto the pile of food that Jade had made.

8. Finally, the group of gingerbread women that Jade had seen earlier yelled, "Stop this madness!"

9. Then the tallest gingerbread man, who was also the town's mayor, declared, "You shall be punished!"

Introductory Words, Transition Words, and Punctuation

F. Fill in the blanks with the appropriate introductory and transition words. Then put the correct punctuation in the boxes.

Introductory and Transition Words

However	Eventually	Finally	Ugh	To make her understand
In fact	After much deliberation	Although	Sadly	Suddenly

_______________, Jade started sobbing and could not talk anymore. _______________, she had realized her mistake and was extremely guilty. _______________, she vowed loudly to never eat any sugary sweets again! _______________, it was not up to Jade to decide her fate.

_______________, the mayor spoke, ☐ _______________ I know why you did this, you will still face the consequences ☐ you will be shown the harsh reality of eating too many sugary sweets! ☐

_______________, the townspeople held up a mirror and asked Jade to look at her teeth. ☐ _______________! What is that on my teeth? ☐ Jade shrieked in horror.

☐ _______________, those black holes in your teeth are cavities and the yellow stuff is plaque, ☐ replied the little mayor.

I love you, Mom!

_______________, Jade decided to do the following ☐ ☐ 1 ☐ brush and floss regularly, ☐ 2 ☐ eat less sugary food, and ☐ 3 ☐ always listen to her mother.

Section 3

Reading

UNIT 1

Koko's Ingenious Navigation

Kiera was happy to make it to the Arctic tundra just before midnight to visit her friend Koko. After greeting Koko's family and exchanging gifts in their igloo, the two girls planned their morning excursion on Koko's snowmobile.

Early the next day, they drank warm tea, packed some snacks, and set out for their excursion. They were having so much fun taking turns driving the snowmobile that they failed to notice the landscape around them. It looked as if there was nothing but plain white snow for miles on end! A thick fog had enveloped them and obscured their vision. Kiera was scared and realized that she had no idea where she was. She screamed at Koko to turn back but her friend continued driving.

After a while, Koko stopped at a big mound of snow and exclaimed, "I know where we are!" She then turned at a right angle and drove for ten minutes before parking in front of her welcoming igloo.

Later, Koko confessed that although she was a little bit afraid, she knew that she would encounter a familiar landmark sooner or later. This confidence stemmed from her childhood training with her grandpa who taught her to always be vigilant and form a close relationship with the land around her. She drew lines in the snow to explain how she viewed the topography of the area – dotted with small and familiar landmarks which are joined together by invisible lines like the grid on graph paper.

"It is kind of like joining the stars in the night sky using straight lines to know where you are," she explained.

Kiera, on the other hand, had grown up in an urban city and had never thought of her neighbourhood this way before. She was enjoying learning about the importance of understanding one's environment from her friend. Koko's instincts had saved them from a dangerous situation. Her navigational strategies worked well in the snow.

Later, Koko said, "The land around us is like a white blanket, yet it's anything but plain. Linear ridges of snow are formed by winds during the Arctic winter. These "sastrugi" are almost like parallel lines running alongside each other and I can gauge my location and reach my destination by driving my snowmobile along these lines."

"Ah, I see! You are using the sastrugi as guidelines," Kiera said with a spark of understanding.

The two friends laughed and talked until they fell asleep in the warm igloo.

A. Circle the answers.

1. Where does Koko live?

   in the Atlantic tundra

   in the Arctic tundra

   in the Antarctic tundra

2. When does Kiera reach Koko's igloo?

   in the morning

   in the afternoon

   at night

3. What mode of transportation do the girls use?

   ice skates

   snowshoes

   a snowmobile

4. What obscures the girls' vision?

   a thick fog

   an iceberg

   a mound of snow

5. How does Kiera feel when she realizes that they are lost?

   scared

   confident

   excited

6. Where has Kiera grown up?

   on a farm

   in a suburb

   in an urban city

B. Fill in the blanks with words from the text.

1. The linear ridges of snow formed by winds during the Arctic winter are called ____________ .

2. Kiera and Koko slept in the warm ____________ .

3. The land around them was anything but ____________ .

4. Koko's ____________ taught her how to navigate her way in nature.

5. Koko drew lines in the snow to explain the area's ____________ .

6. Koko could gauge her ____________ by driving along the lines formed on the snow.

I knew we would find our igloo!

C. Answer the questions.

1. What type of text is this?

____

2. Identify the problem the girls face on their excursion.

____

____

3. What gives Koko confidence to overcome the dangerous situation?

____

____

4. What strategy does Koko use to navigate the snowy tundra?

____

____

D. **Read the following quotes from "Koko's Ingenious Navigation". Then compare and contrast what Koko said about the topography of the land and the night sky.**

About the Topography of the Land:

The land is "dotted with small and familiar landmarks which are joined together by invisible lines like the grid on graph paper."

About the Night Sky:

"It is kind of like joining the stars in the night sky using straight lines to know where you are."

Similarity:

____

____

____

____

Difference:

____

____

____

____

My Notes

____

____

____

____

Section 3 Reading

UNIT 2

The Tale of Tal the Titan

In Old Langshire there lived a legend true.
It spoke of Tal the Titan, a mighty warrior most brave.
He fought off frightful enemies.
There was no soul he would not save.

And so, hearing the screams of villagers one night,
Brave Tal, a living legend true,
Did not for a moment cower in fear,
To save them all he bravely flew.

The frightful enemy, the Fiery Fiends,
Came raging with all their might.
But Tal the Titan, a mighty warrior most brave,
Would not back down without a fight.

The Fiery Fiends, those bandits foul,
In Old Langshire did chaos create.
Destroying crops, and stealing gold,
Those frightening Fiends brought bad fate.

But Tal the Titan, a mighty warrior most brave,
Towered over them and off the Fiery Fiends fled.
Never again would they return,
So the merry villagers a celebration led.

Grateful for his courage and strength,
A golden hero's sword they did give.
"O Tal the Titan, a mighty warrior most brave," cried they.
"Ever shall your noble legend live."

The Tale of
Tal the
Titan...

A. Circle the answers.

1. Where does the legend of Tal the Titan take place?

   in Old Langford

   in Old Langshire

   in Old Langstaff

2. Who is Tal the Titan?

   a mighty villain

   a frightful warrior

   a brave warrior

3. Tal the Titan never cowers in ______ .

   fear

   anger

   fury

4. Who are the Fiery Fiends?

   bandits

   alchemists

   tradesmen

5. What do the Fiery Fiends destroy?

   gold

   crops

   houses

6. What do the Fiery Fiends steal?

   crops

   gold

   rubies

7. The Fiery Fiends are described as ______ .

   frightening

   formidable

   fearful

8. What do the villagers gift to Tal the Titan?

   a chalice

   a royal cloak

   a sword

B. Read "The Tale of Tal the Titan" again. Check the features of a ballad.

A ballad is a narrative poem or song made up of four-line stanzas, with the second and fourth lines rhyming in each stanza. Traditionally, ballads were passed down to the next generation through word of mouth.

1. an abcb rhyme scheme ◯
2. focusing on a single dramatic event ◯
3. no rhyme scheme ◯
4. six lines in each stanza ◯
5. repetition of certain phrases ◯
6. dialogue ◯
7. narration of a story in short stanzas ◯
8. lack of details about the setting ◯
9. usually has a third person perspective ◯

C. Answer the questions.

1. Why is Tal the Titan considered "a mighty warrior most brave"?

____

____

2. Write three traits of Tal's character that the villagers are grateful for.

__________ __________ __________

3. What information about Tal the Titan or his surroundings does the ballad not convey that you would like to know?

____

____

4. Why do you think repetition is an important feature of a ballad?

____

____

D. Read the following stanza from "The Tale of Tal the Titan". Then write two more stanzas continuing the ballad with an alternative ending.

The Fiery Fiends, those bandits foul,
In Old Langshire did chaos create.
Destroying crops, and stealing gold,
Those frightening Fiends brought bad fate.

Remember to rhyme the second and fourth lines of each stanza and include dialogue. Keep the stanzas short.

My Ending:

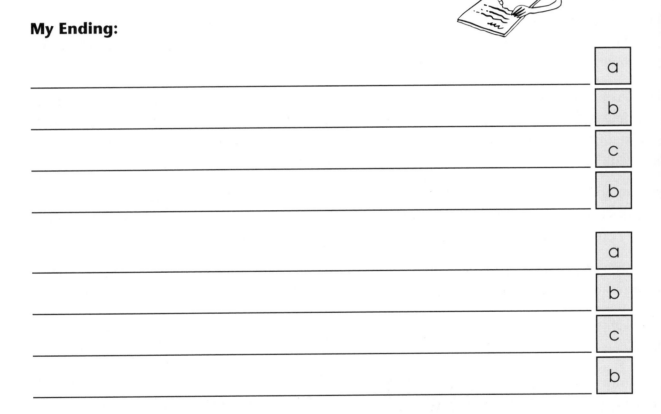

My Notes

UNIT 3

Mr. Jones and the Mysterious Noise

It was a bright and sunny Saturday when Mr. Jones moved in next door. He is an old gentleman with thick-framed glasses and a wiry grey beard. I could see his many belongings: antique chests, a large and tattered painting of a rainforest, and boxes and boxes of old books. The line of movers bringing items into the house was endless! However, there was one item that Mr. Jones refused to let the movers touch. It was covered in a red velvet cloth and he carefully carried it inside himself.

That night, I heard an odd noise coming from Mr. Jones's house and I could not sleep at all! After much deliberation, I decided to investigate this mystery. I wondered, *what could this strange noise be? What could Mr. Jones be hiding?*

The next day, I snuck into his house. He had left the window of his basement unlocked and I crawled inside. I felt around the walls for a light switch and when I finally turned the light on, I gasped!

The basement was like a museum. There were paintings and dioramas of jungles and animals. I was making my way across the room when I heard that strange noise again, coming from upstairs! I walked up the stairs as quietly as I could but then on the last step...the floor beneath my foot creaked! I paused, dead in my tracks, hoping no one was home to hear me.

Suddenly, the door opened and there stood Mr. Jones staring right at me. He asked, "What in goodness gracious are you doing in here?" I gulped and replied, "I...I was just...lost?" He scoffed at my response and pulled me out of his basement.

"Now tell me, what are you really doing here?" asked Mr. Jones. Then I heard the strange noise again, coming from inside the other room.

"What was that? What are you hiding? I'm going to call the police!" I shouted, flinging the door open.

And then I saw it – a large red parrot in an ornate gold cage.

"What are you going to do? Call the police on me for having a pet parrot?" challenged Mr. Jones.

Mr. Jones explained that his parrot had been sick, which was why it was making strange noises. He also told me that he was a retired zoologist and museum curator, and all of the items downstairs were part of his collection. I admitted that it was wrong of me to sneak into his house and that I should have talked to him instead. I learned an important lesson that day: never judge someone before getting to know him or her first!

Now I go over to Mr. Jones's house to visit his parrot every day after school and Mr. Jones and I have become the best of friends!

A. Circle the answers.

1. What are some of Mr. Jones's belongings?

   paintings, monuments, and letters

   paintings, antiques, and magazines

   antiques, paintings, and books

2. How does the protagonist know Mr. Jones?

   They are neighbours.

   They are colleagues.

   They are relatives.

3. How does the protagonist enter Mr. Jones's house?

   He climbs a ladder up to his attic.

   He goes in through the front door.

   He crawls in through the window of his basement.

4. Where is the strange noise coming from?

   upstairs

   downstairs

   the backyard

5. When does the floor creak?

   on the first step

   on the third step

   on the last step

6. What did Mr. Jones work as?

   a zoologist

   a biologist

   a historian

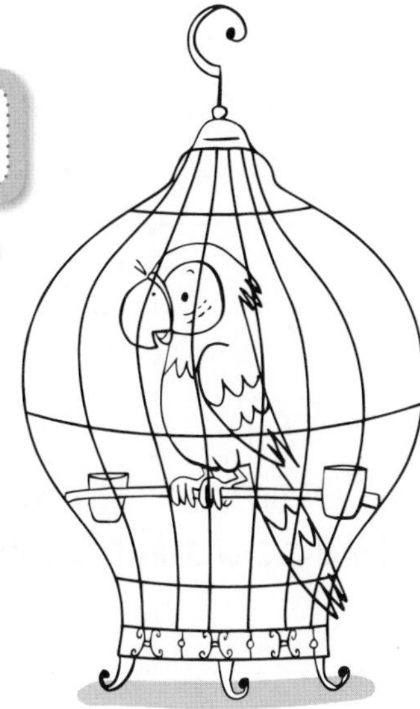

Section 3 Reading

B. Check "T" for the true statements and "F" for the false ones.

		T	F
1.	The protagonist threatens to call a lawyer.	◯	◯
2.	The protagonist does not apologize to Mr. Jones.	◯	◯
3.	Mr. Jones is a retired museum curator.	◯	◯
4.	Mr. Jones's parrot has an ornate red cage.	◯	◯
5.	The dioramas feature jungles and animals.	◯	◯
6.	Mr. Jones hires a lot of movers to help him.	◯	◯
7.	The protagonist has thought a lot before sneaking into Mr. Jones's house.	◯	◯
8.	The protagonist has learned to not judge someone before getting to know him or her.	◯	◯

C. Answer the questions.

A mystery is a story about a mysterious situation that needs to be solved. It usually contains suspense that creates an uncertain mood.

1. What is the protagonist curious about?

____

____

2. Write three sentences from the mystery that build suspense before the protagonist finds out the source of the mysterious noise.

- _______________________________________
- _______________________________________
- _______________________________________

3. What time of day is it when the protagonist sneaks into Mr. Jones's basement? How do you know?

____

____

____

D. **Read the paragraph from the mystery "Mr. Jones and the Mysterious Noise". Explain why Mr. Jones scoffed at the protagonist's response. Then write what your reaction would have been if you were Mr. Jones. Explain your reaction.**

Suddenly, the door opened and there stood Mr. Jones staring right at me. He asked, "What in goodness gracious are you doing in here?" I gulped and replied, "I...I was just...lost?" He scoffed at my response and pulled me out of his basement.

Reason for Mr. Jones's Reaction

____

____

My Reaction

____

____

____

Reason for My Reaction

____

____

____

My Notes

____

____

____

____

UNIT 4

Johnny's Secret

<u>Cast of Characters</u>

Johnny: a teenage boy

Felix: Johnny's younger brother

Mom and Dad: Johnny and Felix's parents

ACT 1

Scene 1

(Curtains rise. Felix and his parents are eating at the dining table. His brother Johnny walks in, looking tired.)

DAD: Johnny, it's time for dinner. Come join us!

JOHNNY: I'm not hungry.

(Johnny leaves and the sound of a door slamming shut is heard off-stage.)

DAD: What has got into him these days? He's been so quiet. He doesn't join family game night. He didn't even want to go out for ice cream yesterday.

MOM: Felix, will you find out what's going on with Johnny?

FELIX: Ugh, do I have to?

ACT 1

Scene 2

(Felix is hiding in the bushes at the park.)

FELIX: Why do I have to spy on him? I'm the younger sibling. Oh, here comes Johnny.

(Johnny enters the park and starts breakdancing. Felix laughs and Johnny stops breakdancing.)

JOHNNY: Hey, who's there?

FELIX: Uh oh, time to get out of here!

JOHNNY: Felix!

(Felix runs off while Johnny chases him.)

ACT 1

Scene 3

(Mom and Dad are at home when Felix and Johnny come barging in. Johnny puts Felix in a headlock.)

FELIX: I caught Johnny dancing! Or more like trying to dance, ha!

DAD: Hey, hey, stop fighting! Johnny, is that why you haven't been acting like yourself these days? You didn't want to tell us that you were dancing?

MOM: Johnny, why didn't you tell us? We will support you, no matter what!

JOHNNY: I guess I was just embarrassed because I'm not good at it.

MOM: Honey, it's alright. Why don't we all go out for ice cream and talk about it?

(Everyone exits and the curtains fall.)

A. Circle the answers.

1. How many acts and scenes are there in the play?

   one act and one scene

   one act and three scenes

   three acts and three scenes

2. Who is the main character?

   Johnny

   Mom

   Dad

3. Where is everyone in the opening scene?

   in the bedroom

   in the dining room

   in the front yard

4. Felix gets caught when ______ .

   he starts laughing

   he starts breakdancing

   he starts yelling out loud

5. How does Mom react to Johnny's secret?

   angrily

   mockingly

   supportively

6. Why does Johnny hide what he is doing?

   He is afraid.

   He is upset.

   He is embarrassed.

B. Answer the questions.

1. Fill in the information about the play.

   Title: ____________________

   Characters: ____________________

   Setting: ____________________

   Conflict: ____________________

   Solution: ____________________

   Dialogue: (Give two examples.)

   ____

   ____

A play is a narrative that is meant to be performed. It is mostly dialogue among characters.

A play is written in acts and scenes.

2. Suggest two props that could be used by the actors for each scene.

Scene 1	Scene 2	Scene 3
________	________	________
________	________	________

A prop is an object used on stage by actors.

3. Write a short dialogue to show what Mom might say as everyone eats ice cream if the play continues.

   MOM: ____________________

   ____

4. What is the message of the play? Explain.

   ____

   ____

5. Write adjectives to show Johnny's character traits.

   Character Traits

   ________ ________

   ________ ________

C. **Write an example of a stage direction from each scene of the play. Then read the dialogue from Scene 3 again and write stage directions for the characters.**

Stage directions guide the actors' movements on stage, and show the actions and behaviour of a character.

Stage Directions

- Scene 1: ______________________

- Scene 2: ______________________

- Scene 3: ______________________

Dialogue from Scene 3:

DAD: Hey, hey, stop fighting! Johnny, is that why you haven't been acting like yourself these days? You didn't want to tell us that you were dancing?

MOM: Johnny, why didn't you tell us? We will support you, no matter what!

Stage Directions

- For Dad: (______________________)

- For Mom: (______________________)

My Notes

UNIT 5

My Wonderful Life

I was born and raised on a farm in the middle of Prince Edward Island. Life on the farm was simple and busy but extremely entertaining. Although we followed the same routine every day, as a young girl, I looked forward to collecting freshly laid eggs before running off to play with the rabbits.

When I was in middle school, I learned to help my parents feed the cows and hens. In my leisure time, I rode Cinnamon, my favourite horse. He galloped around the family ranch while I pretended that I was flying without a care in the world. I shared my deepest secrets with him during the most crucial years of my life.

During high school, my mom decided to home-school my sister and me. My parents always taught us that spending time in nature could tell us a lot about the world we live in. We used to carry our easels, paints, cameras, and little microscopes and study the insects, birds, trees, and frogs in the summer. My sister was more into photography while I liked to sketch a lot. In the cold winter months, we read our favourite books by the great fireplace overlooking the stables. I developed my love for reading and writing fiction during those years.

After high school, I made the toughest decision of my life – I decided to leave my perfect farm life behind for the world of high-rise buildings. I moved to New York to obtain my Bachelor of Arts degree in English Literature.

At first, it was overwhelming – there were so many sights and sounds to take in and life in the the city moved fast. I soon found my rhythm; however, I still missed the simple pleasures of my life on the farm. My family visited once a year and when they were gone, I was enveloped by nostalgia and homesickness. But I trudged on, determined to find my own voice through writing. During this time, falling in love with writing children's books saved me from loneliness.

Years later, my parents passed away and my sister moved to Europe to pursue her own dreams. Life on the farm seemed like a lost memory. Sensing my despair, my husband tried his best to recreate a happy life for me by planting a small rooftop garden atop our apartment complex and helping me raise our two beautiful sons. So here I am, an old lady with two adult sons and three little grandchildren.

Now, as I sit in this busy café with my laptop, I feel grateful for the amazing childhood I had, the many learning opportunities I was presented with along the way, and the people I love. I am sure that my life will come full circle and my plans of retiring to my beloved farm will materialize in the next few years. Until then, I sip coffee and watch people going about their own lives.

A. Circle the answers.

1. Where was the writer raised?

   on Prince Edward Island

   in British Columbia

   in New York

2. What was the writer's horse called?

   Cardamom

   Cinnamon

   Cayenne

3. What did the writer study in university?

   English Literature

   Political Science

   French Literature

4. How often did the writer's family visit her?

   weekly

   monthly

   annually

5. What saved the writer from loneliness?

   reading

   writing

   studying

6. Where did the writer's sister move to?

   Prince Edward Island

   New York

   Europe

7. How many grandchildren does the writer have?

   one

   two

   three

8. What does the writer like to drink at the café?

   hot chocolate

   tea

   coffee

B. Answer the questions.

1. What type of text is this? Write one feature of this text form.

____

____

2. Why did the writer move to New York?

____

____

3. Which stage of her life does the writer write most about? Why?

____

____

____

C. Write one event for each stage in the writer's life.

TIMELINE	LIFE EVENTS
Childhood	
Middle School	
High School	
University	
Post University	

D. **Write examples from the writer's life that show the application of the quote below. Then write about the importance of nature in your own life.**

1.

2.

3.

4.

"*My parents always taught us that spending time in nature could tell us a lot about the world we live in.*"

The Importance of Nature in My Life:

My Notes

UNIT 6

Pablo Picasso

Early Life

- liked drawing from an early age
- had his first formal academic art training from his father in figure drawing and oil painting
- attended carpenter schools throughout his childhood
- classwork suffered due to his interest in art
- disliked formal instruction and never finished his college-level course at the Academy of Arts in Madrid

Family History

- born in the city of Málaga in Spain
- eldest child of the family
- came from a middle-class background
- his father José Ruiz Blasco was a painter, professor of art, and curator of a local museum

Pablo Picasso (1881 – 1973)

Major Accomplishments

- one of the most famous artists of the 20th century
- co-founded the Cubist movement
- used various styles and techniques in his work
- started painting when he was 7 and produced his first oil paintings by the age of 13
- talented painter, sculptor, poet, ceramic artist, and stage designer
- his works are sold worldwide for millions of dollars

Famous Quotes

"Everything you can imagine is real."

"Inspiration exsists but it has to find you working."

"Every child is an artist. The problem is how to remain an artist once he grows up."

Struggles

- struggled with poverty, tragedy, and relationships
- lost his seven-year-old sister in 1895
- his closest friend committed suicide
- suffered from dyslexia
- could not sell enough of his works to financially support himself initially

Interesting Fact

- Picasso's mother reported that his first word was "piz, piz", the short form of "lápiz", which is the Spanish word for "pencil"!

A. Circle the answers.

1. What was Picasso's father?

   a professor of art

   a carpenter

   a stage designer

2. Who trained Picasso in figure drawing?

   his instructor

   his father

   his friend

3. What role did Picasso play in the Cubist movement?

   He founded it.

   He co-founded it.

   He ended it.

4. What did Picasso struggle with?

   poverty, tragedy, and relationships

   poverty, sickness, and lack of talent

   poverty, anaemia, and rejection

5. What did Picasso suffer from?

   dyslexia

   dementia

   anorexia

Section 3 Reading

B. Answer the questions.

1. How did Picasso's father influence his career?

2. What are some of the events that show Picasso's creativity and talent?

3. Did Picasso immediately become successful with his art? Explain.

4. What is the significance of Picasso's first word?

C. Write an example for each text feature from the graphic organizer about Pablo Picasso.

A graphic organizer visually displays relationships among facts, concepts, or ideas, often employing the use of text boxes to organize information. It can help in writing, studying, planning, and decision-making.

Text Feature	**Example**
1. Title:	
2. Subheading:	
3. Illustration:	
4. Text Box:	
5. Variety of Fonts:	
6. Variety of Font Sizes:	
7. Short Phrase:	

D. Read Pablo Picasso's quotes again and answer the questions.

1 "Everything you can imagine is real."

2 "Inspiration exists, but it has to find you working."

3 "Every child is an artist. The problem is how to remain an artist once he grows up."

1. Do you agree that art makes things you imagine real? Why or why not?

___

___

___

2. Do you think that hard work is just as important as inspiration?

___

___

___

3. What do you think Picasso meant by quote (3)?

___

___

___

My Notes

___

___

___

___

UNIT 7

The World's Most Unusual Animals

You have probably heard about the dumbo octopus, springbok, and maybe even the gerenuk, dugong, and the fossa. But have you heard of the unusual animals described in the table below?

The World's Most Unusual Animals

Animal	Habitat	Distinctive Feature
Capybara	• lives in the rainforests and savannahs of South America • likes to live near water	• has partially-webbed feet and a hippo-like body • a full grown male is around 135 cm long and can weigh as much as 65 kg • looks like an overgrown guinea pig
Jerboa	• lives in hot deserts • is found throughout Northern Africa and Asia	• has a long tail and powerful legs that help it jump up to 3 m in one leap • may never drink water • gets its moisture from the plants and insects it eats
Okapi	• prefers very dense tropical rainforests and riverbeds • found in the Ituri Rainforest in Central Africa	• looks like a mix between a horse and a zebra • has reddish-brown fur with white stripes on its rump and hind legs
Tomato Frog	• lives only in Madagascar near the coast of Southeast Africa • lives in marshes and still-water channels	• bright reddish-orange in colour • inflates its body into what looks like a big, red tomato when threatened

Guanaco	• lives in deserts, grasslands, and mountains in South America	• camel-like appearance • has light or reddish-brown fur with a white underside • has large doe-like brown eyes, a streamlined and energetic body, and a short tail
Long-nosed Chimaera 	• lives in temperate and tropical waters around the world at depths of 200 m to 2000 m	• looks like a slimy, scaleless sea creature with a serpent's tail, a shark-like body, and a pointy duck-bill • has rodent-like teeth

As some of the unusual animals require special living conditions, they can only be found in very specific parts of the world. Human activities such as hunting, littering, and deforestation threaten the survival of these strange creatures. Therefore, we should all make efforts to conserve their habitats and protect them from harm!

A. Circle the answers.

1. Which of the animals are described in the text?

   gerenuk, jerboa, and octopus

   capybara, jerboa, and okapi

   guanaco, guinea pig, and springbok

2. How does the jerboa stay hydrated?

   by drinking water

   by swimming

   by ingesting plants and insects

3. The okapi has white stripes on its ______ .

   rump and underside

   rump and hind legs

   underside and hind legs

4. Which animal is found only in Madagascar?

   the jerboa

   the okapi

   the tomato frog

B. Answer the questions.

A table represents data in rows and columns. A table has a title, subheadings, and facts. Short phrases and bullet points are used in place of sentences.

1. What type of text is this? Suggest two additional subheadings to describe the animals.

____

____

2. How do the jerboa's powerful legs help it?

____

____

3. Where does the long-nosed chimaera live?

____

____

4. Which of the animals described in the text do you find most unusual? Why?

____

____

C. Compare and contrast the animals described in the text by completing the table below.

Similarities and Differences between the World's Most Unusual Animals

Animal	Similarity	Difference
Capybara and Okapi		
________ and ________	live in deserts	
________ and ________	reddish-brown appearance	

D. In the table "The World's Most Unusual Animals", visual comparisons to more well-known animals are made to explain the appearance of some of the unusual species. Write the comparisons to complete the flash cards.

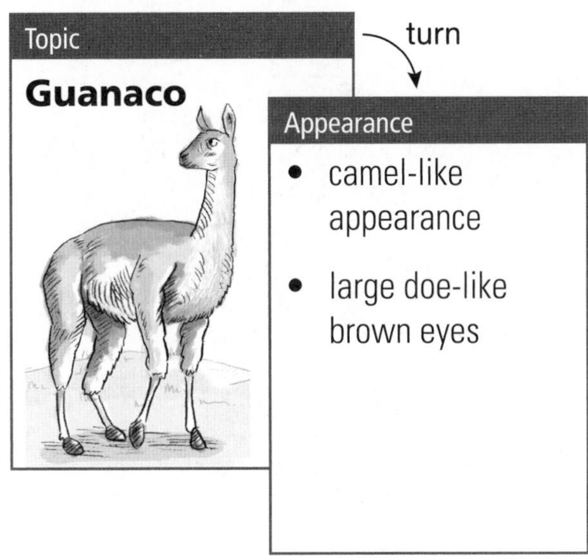

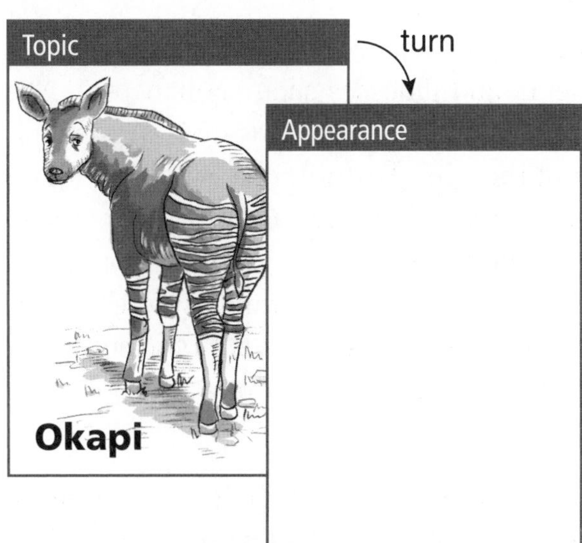

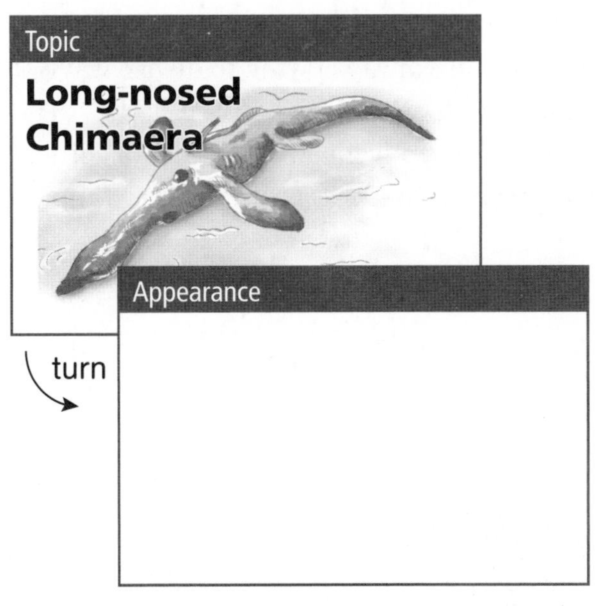

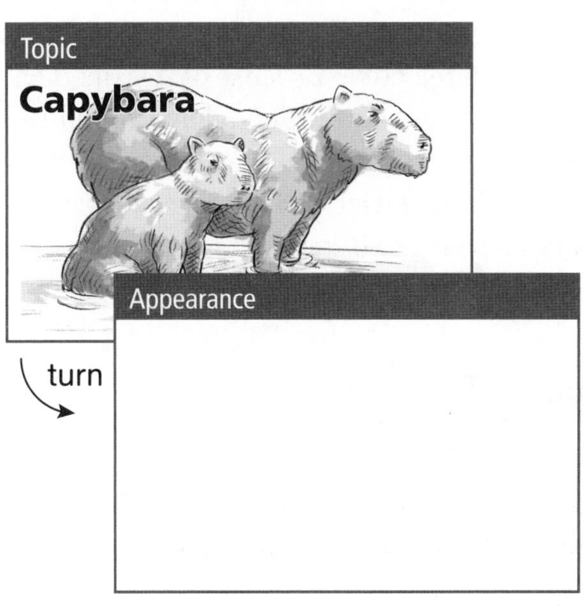

My Notes

Section 3 Reading

UNIT 8 Tooth-in-eye Surgery

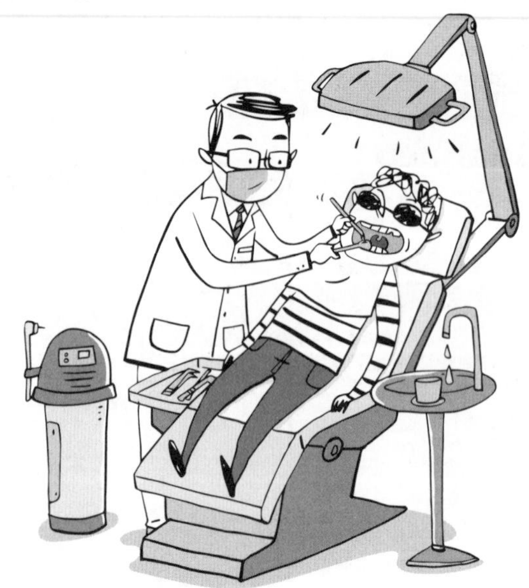

Blindness can occur for many reasons, including accidents and illnesses such as diabetes. Another cause of blindness is related to physical problems with parts of the eye. For instance, blindness can occur when the cornea becomes damaged. The cornea is the clear, dome-shaped covering over the pupil and iris that helps refract light, allowing us to see. However, when opaque scar tissue forms on the cornea due to damage, light cannot pass through it. This obstructs the patient's eyesight.

In the past, the standard procedure for attempting to restore eyesight to a patient with a damaged cornea was to transplant a healthy cornea from a cadaver. However, transplantation has side effects. When any organ or body part given by a donor is transplanted into the recipient, there is a chance that it will be rejected. Because of this, medical researchers are always trying to devise ways of having the recipient's own body involved in the manufacturing of essential "spare parts". The tooth-in-eye technique is one such attempt. It is an innovative and advanced procedure of corneal transplantation in which a new cornea is created using the patient's own tooth. It is a complex surgery involving two stages:

Stage 1

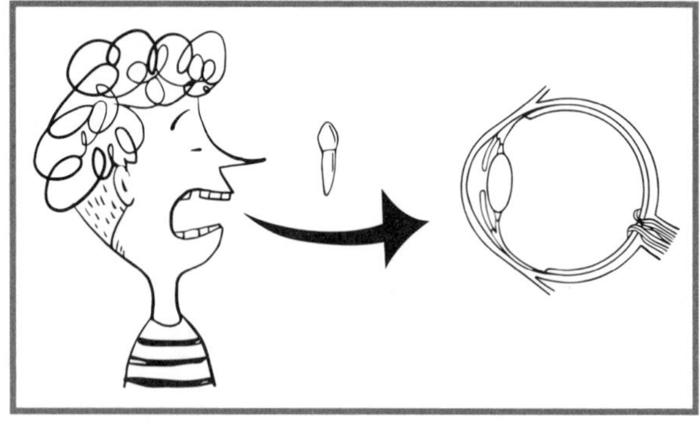

1. One of the patient's canine teeth and some adjacent bone and jaw ligaments are taken out.
2. These are then shaped into a cube and a hole is drilled into the tooth.
3. A tiny plastic corneal device is implanted into the hole. This amalgam of human tooth, bone, tissue, and artificial cornea is called an "optical cylinder".
4. The optical cylinder is placed into the patient's own cheek for several months and human tissue grows over it during this time.

Stage 2

1. The damaged eye is cleared of scar tissue.
2. An opening is made in the patient's damaged eye.
3. The optical cylinder, which is now a piece of living human tissue, is removed from the patient's cheek.
4. The optical cylinder is implanted into the patient's eyeball.

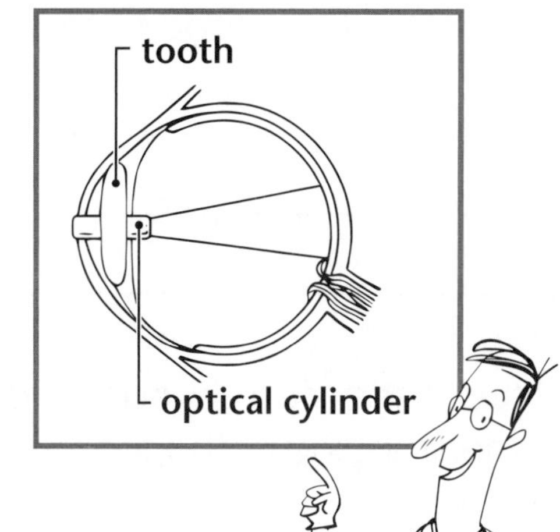

After this procedure, light enters the optical cylinder which refracts light like a cornea, thereby restoring vision to the patient!

A. Circle the answers.

1. Blindness can result from ______ .

   accidents

   a decayed tooth

   emotional issues

2. What is the clear, dome-shaped covering over the pupil and iris called?

   retina

   cornea

   eyeball

3. How does the cornea help us see?

   by reflecting light

   by refracting light

   by absorbing light

4. Where is the optical cylinder placed in Stage 1?

   in the patient's damaged eye

   in the patient's teeth

   in the patient's cheek

5. What does the optical cylinder replace?

   the pupil

   the iris

   the cornea

6. How long does it take for human tissue to grow over the optical cylinder?

   several days

   several months

   several years

B. Answer the questions.

1. Explain how damage to the cornea can result in blindness.

2. Rewrite the steps in each stage in the form of paragraphs to show your understanding of the tooth-in-eye procedure.

Stage 1

Stage 2

C. Write four features of the text. Then write the purpose of each.

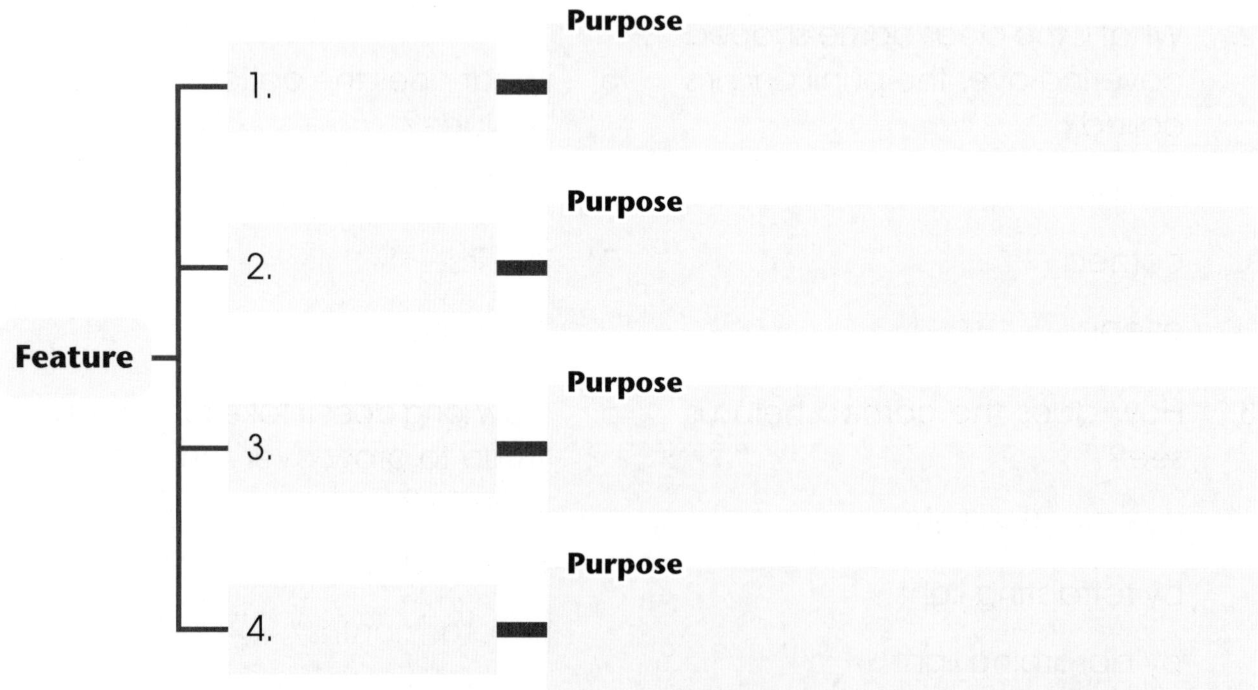

D. Read the text "Tooth-in-eye Surgery" again. Then write about the drawbacks of a corneal transplant from an organ donor and why the tooth-in-eye procedure is preferred.

Drawbacks of Corneal Transplantation through Organ Donation

Benefits of Tooth-in-eye Surgery

My Notes

UNIT 9 The History of Avian Flu

History | Chapter 8

The History of Avian Flu

What is Avian Flu?

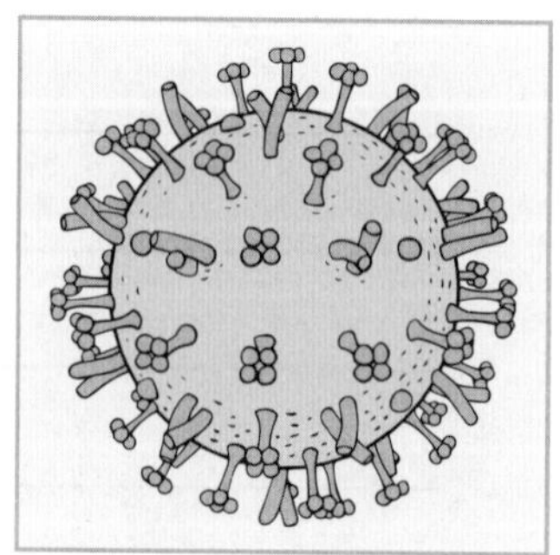
Influenza A virus

Avian influenza is also known as avian flu or bird flu. It is a viral infection that affects birds. Although there are different strains of influenza, and Influenza A is adapted to birds, it can also spread to the human population. Since the beginning of the 20th century, the flu has been one of our greatest causes for concern.

Major Outbreaks and Impacts:

Spanish Flu

One of the largest pandemics of all time is the 1918 "Spanish Flu" (so-called because this flu, spread worldwide by soldiers returning home after World War One, was most widely reported in Spain, where newspapers were not subject to wartime censorship as Spain was not involved in the war). This pandemic killed around 50 to 100 million people between 1918 and 1919. Studies carried out on the bodies of WWI soldiers and an Inuit woman preserved in the Alaskan permafrost confirmed that they had been infected with the H1N1 virus.

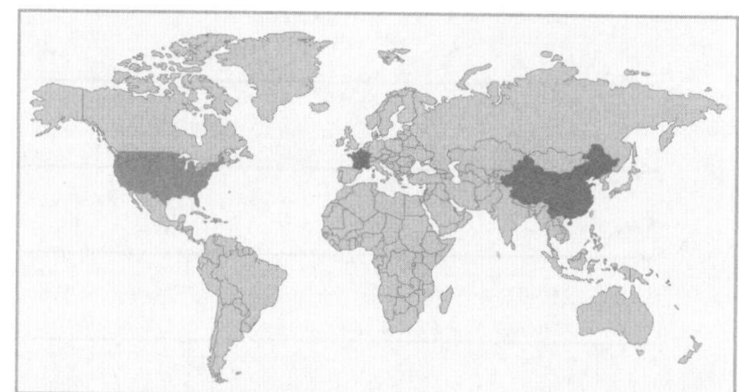
Fig. 1.1 There are three possible origins of the Spanish Flu.

P. 256

A. Circle the answers.

1. Avian influenza is also known as ______.

   chicken flu

   cow flu

   bird flu

2. The Spanish Flu killed around ______ people.

   5 to 10 million

   50 to 100 million

   50 to 100 billion

3. What type of virus was found in the bodies of WWI soldiers?

   H1N1

   H3N2

   H5N1

Asian Flu

Numerous avian flu outbreaks occurred later in the 20th century. The 1957 "Asian Flu", caused by the influenza A subtype H2N2 virus, claimed between 1 and 2 million lives, and in 1968, the "Hong Kong Flu" pandemic, caused by the influenza A subtype H3N2 virus, resulted in an estimated 1 to 4 million deaths worldwide.

Hong Kong was in the news in 1997 when the avian flu virus H5N1 infected 18 people and eventually claimed six lives. In 2003, it claimed one life in Hong Kong.

Other Outbreaks:

Viruses are always mutating, making it difficult for human bodies to develop immunity to them. Also, the world is becoming more globalized as people travel more and more. These are some of the reasons why viral illnesses can be so contagious. In 2003, another strain of the virus, H7N7, infected numerous people in the Netherlands. In 2004, the H5N1 and H7N3 strains caused deaths in Vietnam and Thailand, as well as a few cases of infection in Canada.

Nowadays, disease-control centres are making avian flu their top priority as the world becomes more globalized and different strains of the virus are detected.

In the meantime, you can protect yourself by staying away from wild birds, washing your hands thoroughly, and disinfecting surfaces where raw and cooked poultry is handled. Also, poultry should be cooked at a temperature of at least 70 degrees Celsius to kill the virus.

* Source of Map for Fig. 1.1:
"War in History: Journal of Public Health Policy"

4. Which pandemic occurred in 1968?

   the "Spanish Flu" pandemic

   the "Asian Flu" pandemic

   the "Hong Kong Flu" pandemic

5. Which pandemic was the most fatal?

   the "Spanish Flu"

   the "Asian Flu"

   the "Hong Kong Flu"

6. Who is making avian flu their top priority?

   disease-control centres

   doctors

   poultry chefs

B. Answer the questions.

1. Why was the "Spanish Flu" so widespread after World War One?

____

____

2. It is predicted that if there is an outbreak of influenza in the future, it will be much more widespread than in the past. Read the text again and give two reasons for this prediction.

Reason 1: ______________________________

____

Reason 2: ______________________________

____

3. How can you protect yourself from contracting avian flu?

____

____

____

C. Check to show the features of the text. Then fill in the blanks.

Features of the Text

- ◯ captions
- ◯ illustrations
- ◯ subheadings
- ◯ arrows
- ◯ facts
- ◯ source

A historical non-fiction text includes facts (not opinions) and uses formal language. The purpose of a historical non-fiction text is to provide information.

Another feature that can be added to the text is ______________.

D. **Read the text "The History of Avian Flu" again. Write three facts from the text.**

1. ______________________________

____

2. ______________________________

____

3. ______________________________

____

E. **Read the quote from the text. Then answer the question.**

"Since the beginning of the 20th century, the flu has been one of our greatest causes for concern."

Do you agree with this statement? Why or why not?

____

____

____

____

____

My Notes

____

____

____

____

UNIT 10

Flight Safety Manual

Before takeoff, all flights require the passengers to carefully study the safety manual placed in front of their seats. Doing this can save lives in the case of an emergency!

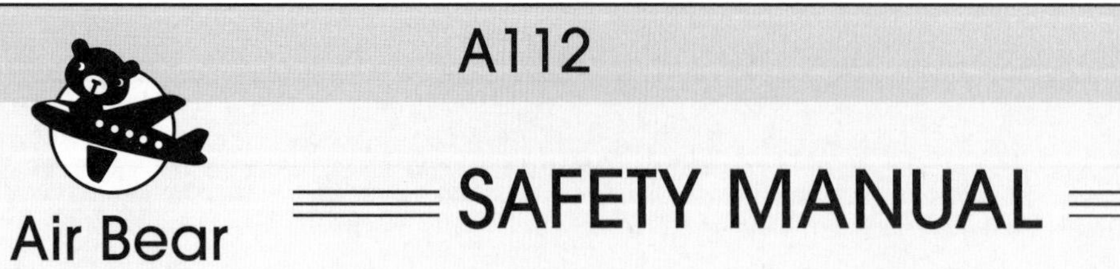

Welcome aboard!

This is the safety manual for Air Bear A112. Please settle down and carefully go through the step-by-step instructions that can help you in case of an emergency.

A This section shows you the proper ways of stowing your luggage, sitting in an upright position, and buckling your seat belt during takeoff and landing.

B This section shows the steps to follow in case of a lack of oxygen during the flight.

C This section shows the detailed layout and locations of exits on this aircraft and the procedures that are used in the event of an emergency landing.

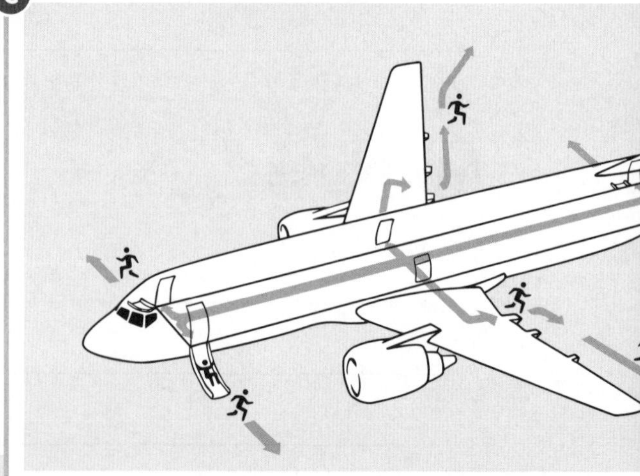

Figure 1.1 Locations of Emergency Exits

Inflight smoking is strictly prohibited.

A. Circle the answers.

1. What type of text is this?

   a diagram

   a manual

   an advertisement

2. Which is necessary before takeoff and landing?

   taking out your luggage

   reclining your seat

   buckling your seat belt

3. Which section shows the necessary steps to follow in case of a lack of oxygen?

   Section A

   Section B

   Section C

4. Where can luggage be stowed?

   in unoccupied seats

   in overhead compartments

   in seat pockets

5. What information does Figure 1.1 give?

   locations of emergency exits

   locations of oxygen masks

   locations of washrooms

6. Which item is not allowed off the plane in case of an emergency landing?

   luggage

   clothing

   cell phone

B. Draw lines to match the features of the "Flight Safety Manual".

A manual is a graphic text. The purpose of a manual is to provide instructions. A manual can tell you how to operate a machine, learn a subject, follow safety rules, and much more.

Feature	Example
title •	• (airplane logo)
sections •	• A, B, C
explanation •	• (no luggage symbol)
symbol •	• Figure 1.1
logo •	• A112 Safety Manual
diagram •	• "This section shows the steps to follow in case of lack of oxygen during the flight."

C. Answer the questions.

1. When should passengers look at the flight safety manual? Why?

___

___

2. What does this diagram demonstrate?

___

___

3. Explain the steps involved in putting on oxygen masks for adults and children.

___

___

___

D. **Write the letters to match the safety features of A112 with their purposes. Then draw two symbols from the manual and write what they mean.**

Purpose of Safety Feature

1. to prevent or reduce the impact of an accident ◯
2. to ensure that the passengers feel comfortable in their seats ◯
3. to store the luggage in a safe place ◯
4. to provide an exit in case of an emergency ◯
5. to help passengers reach the ground quickly ◯
6. to provide oxygen ◯

Safety Feature

A oxygen mask
B seat belt
C adjustable seat
D emergency door
E slides instead of stairs
F overhead luggage compartment

Manuals contain symbols because they are easy to understand and take up less space. A manual has to be informative, clear, and concise.

	Symbol	**Meaning**
1.		______________________
2.		______________________

My Notes

____

____

____

____

UNIT 11 Return of the International Triathlon

THE SMART DAILY NEWS

August 28, 2019

RETURN OF THE INTERNATIONAL TRIATHLON

By Volley Runner

The host city of the International Triathlon has been announced. The games are finally returning to North America in 2020 after Sydney, Australia hosted them in 2017. Next year, they will take place in Toronto, and this will mark the third Triathlon hosted by Canada. And for the first time ever, the opening and closing ceremonies for the International Triathlon will be held indoors at the Scarborough Sports Arena.

Last month, before bidding for the chance to host the games, Toronto residents were asked in a referendum whether they would accept the responsibilities of the host city should it win its bid. Sixty-four percent of the residents accepted the challenge. It is the first time such a referendum has been successful. Toronto won the bidding process to host the Triathlon to be held on June 22, 2020.

Upon being interviewed, the Canadian Triathlon Team pledged, "We will win the most gold medals at the 2020 International Triathlon!" To achieve this lofty goal, Get in Gear 2020 has been launched. It is a collaborative effort supported by all of Canada's national sports federations. The focus is to provide additional resources and a high-performance program for Canadian athletes and coaches to help Canadian athletes reach the utmost success in 2020.

The Canadian Triathlon Team pledging to win the most gold medals in the 2020 games

Other preparations that are underway include: the incorporation of a new subway line in order to better host the influx of athletes and tourists during the games; the expansion of the Downtown Sports Stadium with upgraded state-of-the-art sports equipment; and the formation and recruitment of organizations and volunteers to ensure a smooth flow of events.

A. Circle the answers.

1. What is the title of the newspaper article?

   Return of the International Triathlon

   The Smart Daily News

   Volley Runner

2. Where were the International Triathlon Games held in 2017?

   in North America

   in Toronto

   in Sydney

3. How many International Triathlons have been previously hosted in Canada?

   one

   two

   three

4. What percentage of Toronto's residents accepted the challenge?

   thirty-eight percent

   forty-six percent

   sixty-four percent

5. When will the Triathlon be held?

   on June 20, 2020

   on June 22, 2020

   on June 24, 2020

6. What program has been launched to help Canadian athletes?

   Get in Shape 2020

   Get in Gear 2020

   Get the Medals 2020

7. Which place is being expanded and upgraded for the Triathlon?

   Scarborough Sports Arena

   Downtown Sports Stadium

   Toronto Triathlon Stadium

8. How many athletes make up the Canadian Triathlon Team?

   three

   four

   five

B. Answer the questions.

1. How was Toronto selected to host the International Triathlon Games?

____

____

2. What is the purpose of Get in Gear 2020?

____

____

____

3. How is Toronto preparing to host the International Triathlon?

____

____

____

____

____

____

swimming
cycling
running
International Triathlon

C. Write or circle to give information about the features of the newspaper article.

Name of the Newspaper: ______________________________

Date: ______________________________

Headline: ______________________________

Byline: ______________________________

Introduction: Paragraph(s) 1 2 3 4

Body: Paragraph(s) 1 2 3 4

A newspaper article discusses current events on topics of interest to the public. It is part of a newspaper, is generally written in columns, and contains related pictures with captions.

Caption: ______________________________

Quote: ______________________________

D. **Read the newspaper article "Return of the International Triathlon" again. Then write your thoughts on the question below in the form of an opinion column.**

Come up with a title for your article and remember to think critically about the information you read.

NEWS

Would you want your city to host the International Triathlon?

THE SMART DAILY NEWS

August 29, 2019

By

Triathlon

swimming → cycling → running

My Notes

A. Circle the answers.

1. A short story can usually be read ______ .

   in one sitting

   over many days

   over weeks

2. How many lines are there in a stanza of a ballad?

   three

   four

   six

3. How were ballads traditionally passed down to the next generation?

   textually

   orally

   visually

4. Which of the following is not a feature of a ballad?

   abcb rhyme scheme

   dialogue

   no rhyme scheme

5. What does suspense create in a story?

   a cheerful mood

   an uncertain mood

   an indifferent mood

6. A play is meant to be ______ .

   performed

   watched on screen

   read in a book

7. A prop is an object used ______ .

   off stage by directors

   on stage by actors

   off stage by actors

8. Stage directions guide the actors' ______ on stage.

   dialogue

   language

   movements

9. In an autobiography, the writer's life events appear in ______ .

   reverse order

   the order of importance

   chronological order

10. Which type of text visually displays relationships among facts, concepts, or ideas?

    a graphic organizer

    a diorama

    a newspaper article

11. A graphic organizer can help in writing, studying, planning, or ______ .

proofreading

reading

decision-making

Plan A
yes no
Plan B Plan C

12. A table represents data in ______ .

diagrams

rows and columns

paragraphs

13. Which is not a feature of a table?

bullet points

subheadings

dialogue

14. Which is a feature of a diagram?

arrows

columns

instructions

15. A historical non-fiction text does not ______ .

include opinions

include facts

provide information

16. What type of language does a historical non-fiction text use?

informal

formal

figurative

17. A manual is not a/an ______ text.

graphic

literary

informational

How to Build a
Boat:
steps
1.
2.
3.

18. The purpose of a manual is to provide ______ .

an evaluation

data

instructions

19. What do newspaper articles discuss?

current events

academic subjects

literature

20. A newspaper article is generally written ______ .

with subheadings

in bullet points

in columns

Sports Today
A Basketball Star

B. Read the short story and write "T" for the true statements and "F" for the false ones.

The Mermaid's Melody

Three nights ago, Dorian set out on a voyage to an obscure archipelago in the southern sea to find the Lost Treasure of Rastus. He had heard stories about the sea – how nefarious the rock formations were, and how it was haunted by strange sounds and voices. But Dorian was a skilled helmsman, an esteemed navigator, and the respected captain of The Titan – and he did not put stock in such ridiculous stories.

This is why when Dorian heard a gentle melody sounding in his ears, he was half convinced he was imagining it. But it persisted, and his crewmen heard it too. They stopped their work and looked out into the distance as the singing echoed all around them. Dorian was spellbound by the soft melody. *Surely such a beautiful voice could not mean danger*, he thought.

"I must follow that voice and then we will veer back for the treasure," he told his crewmen. "We are changing course. Prepare to head east!"

"Captain, the east is perilously strewn with rocks! It isn't safe," a crewman insisted.

But Dorian took no heed of the warnings and stubbornly turned the ship due east. So they sailed into the night, letting the soft, unrelenting melody guide them. Dorian was a man possessed with the need to capture that beautiful, unearthly voice.

So entranced was Dorian by the voice that he did not take notice of the treacherous rock formation ahead of him. Distantly, he heard the shouts of his crew, but their voices were drowned out by the song in his ears. He could see the bearer of the voice now. She sat atop the dark, jagged rocks, scornful – her scaly, gleaming fish tail swaying back and forth.

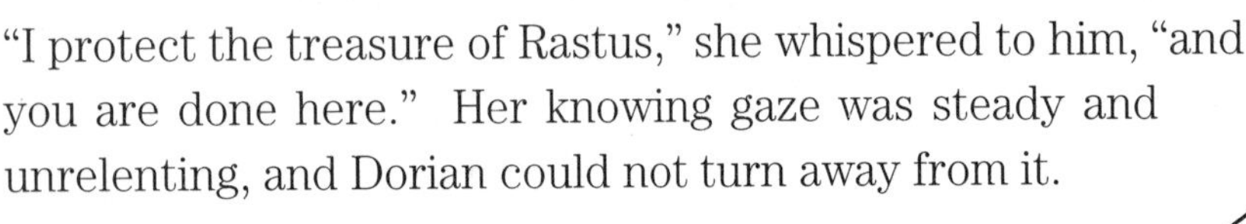

"I protect the treasure of Rastus," she whispered to him, "and you are done here." Her knowing gaze was steady and unrelenting, and Dorian could not turn away from it.

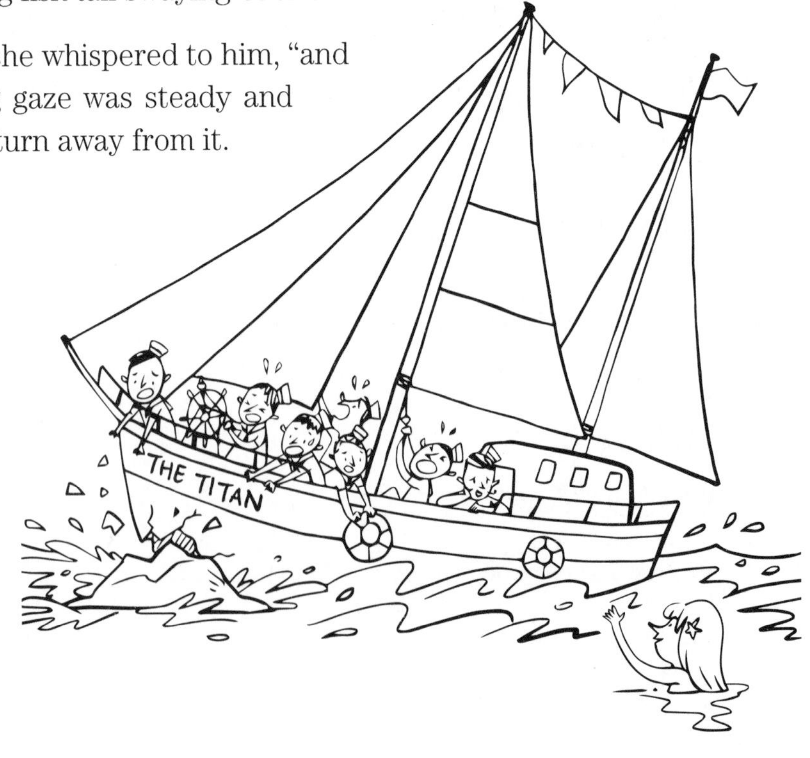

No one will ever believe I saw a mermaid, Dorian thought, as the ship went crashing into the rock. But it did not matter anyway; within minutes, the ship would sink to the depths of the sea, taking Dorian and his crew with it and leaving behind only stories of what happened there.

1. Dorian sets out on a voyage to an obscure archipelago in the northern sea. ____

2. Dorian wants to find the Lost Treasure of Rastus. ____

3. The southern sea has nefarious rock formations. ____

4. Dorian is a skilled crewman. ____

5. Dorian is the respected captain of The Titan. ____

6. The crewmen do not hear the gentle melody. ____

7. Dorian tells his crew to head west toward the voice. ____

8. The east is perilously strewn with rock. ____

9. The Titan crashes into a treacherous rock formation. ____

C. Answer the questions.

1. Why does Dorian believe he is imagining the melody?

____

____

2. Write three adjectives you would use to describe Dorian.

__________ __________ __________

3. Why does the mermaid lure Dorian and his crew toward the rocks?

____

____

4. Describe the mermaid in your own words.

____

5. Do you think this short story has a satisfying ending? Why or why not?

____

____

D. Check the features of a newspaper article. Then fill in the blanks with information from "The Mermaid's Melody".

Features of a Newspaper Article

- newspaper name ○
- arrows ○
- headline ○
- byline ○
- text box ○
- date ○
- columns ○
- quote ○
- image ○
- caption ○

THE SMART NEWS

February 11, 2019

Lost at Sea

By Madeline Louis

The search continues for the lost voyagers of The Titan, a ship helmed by the respected captain D__________, who is described as a skilled h__________ and an esteemed n__________. Striving for fame and glory, the captain and his crew set out to an a__________ in the s__________ sea last week to find the legendary Lost Treasure of R__________. The area is notorious for its nefarious r__________ f__________ that make sailing the water dangerous.

The Smart News interviewed a local historian to gauge his thoughts on the tragic ordeal and he had this to say: "Some have described the southern sea as being haunted by strange sounds and v__________. Others have said there is a m__________ who resides there, protecting the lost treasure. She sings a soft m__________, luring greedy sailors away from the archipelago toward their demise."

Though there is nothing to substantiate these fictitious claims, officials advise to keep away from the southern sea. For now, the search for The Titan continues.

The Titan on the day of its departure

E. Read the ballad and answer the questions.

The Lost Treasure of Rastus

There once lived a king named Rastus –
Born of a water God was he.
He hoarded gold and precious gems,
Burying them on a rocky isle in the southern sea.

To greet his fortune in the afterlife,
Was the only thought that gave King Rastus pleasure.
So, his grateful friend, the loyal mermaid, said:
"Dear King, I vow to always protect your treasure."

And so, the fierce and faithful mermaid,
By the treacherous rocks dwells forever,
Using her voice to lure voyagers down,
One by one they fall, returning home – never.

1. Write three traits of the mermaid's character.

_______________ _______________ _______________

2. Circle the feature of a ballad that is not included in "The Lost Treasure of Rastus".

dialogue | four-line stanzas | repetition
abcb rhyme scheme | third person perspective | single dramatic event

3. What information not given in "The Lost Treasure of Rastus" would you like to know about?

____

____

Section 4

Writing

UNIT 1 Word Choice

Ayden's "One Flowery Day"

Roy and Donna had been touring the art gallery for what felt like hours before they came across the painting they had come to see – Ayden's "One Flowery Day".

"Isn't it breathtaking?" Roy asked, awe-struck. "The vibrant colours take us on a journey to a heavenly garden full of light, hope, and promise," he mused. "The majestic yellow flowers stroll above the horizon, almost touching the bright, bountiful blue skies. And the sky itself is full of skilfully dotted clouds as white as cotton, with rays of shimmering sunlight peeking through, softly illuminating the dancing daffodils."

Donna nodded absently. She was preoccupied with the information board next to the painting that outlined the Current and Future Sales Projections for the artist's paintings. "There was a small dip in the number of paintings sold in the years 2015 and 2016, though consumer interest in Ayden's paintings and his popularity with the public has increased steadily in the last few years," she said assertively. "'One Flowery Day', in particular, has been received well by critics."

Roy, still enraptured by the painting, continued with his praise. "Forget about that! Look at the detail in this art! The clouds, flowers, leaves, and grass are full of vivid shades and hues, yet the houses are slathered with a dreary tone of dull, dingy grey...making them seem abandoned and insignificant to us," Roy considered thoughtfully. "The transition of darkness into light gives the sky a soft, dream-like focus. It is as if Ayden wants our eyes to travel upward with the flight of the enchanting butterflies."

Donna did not seem fazed by his flowery speech. "Well, the technique behind his brushstrokes and his use of oil-paints logically appeal to art collectors and the public alike, according to most surveys. The global demand for Ayden's contemporary style paintings, following the recent surge of his popularity on social media platforms, will continue to increase. There is a high probability that

"One Flowery Day" will earn him international fame, which will only further his profitability."

Roy just shook his head, sighing and smiling at his friend. "Donna, can't you just enjoy this great work of art without being so technical about it?"

A. Read the text. Then write three examples each of the verbs, adjectives, and adverbs used in the text to identify the specified word choice.

Language can be descriptive, technical, and more.

Word choice refers to the use of vocabulary by the writer to convey a specific idea to the reader. Effective word choice is mainly achieved through the use of appropriate nouns, verbs, adjectives, and adverbs.

1. Word Choice for Descriptive Language

Verb	**Adjective**	**Adverb**
e.g. nodded	e.g. vibrant	e.g. skilfully
____________	____________	____________
____________	____________	____________
____________	____________	____________

2. Word Choice for Technical Language

Verb	**Adjective**	**Adverb**
e.g. sold	e.g. global	e.g. assertively
____________	____________	____________
____________	____________	____________
____________	____________	____________

The language of a text – formal, informal, positive, or negative – determines the choice of words.

To convey the intended message in your writing, the purpose and the audience of the text should be kept in mind to make the proper word choice.

Examples

Word Choice for:

- Formal Language
  I would be honoured to pay you a visit.
- Informal Language
  I'll come over to your place soon.
- Positive Language
  Sure! I would be thrilled to have you over.
- Negative Language
  No way! It is not a good idea.

B. Write "Formal", "Informal", "Positive", or "Negative" to identify the type of language shown by the choice of words in each text. Underline the words or phrases that show the use of word choice.

1. To Whom It May Concern,

   I am writing to inform you of my early retirement from Techni Mart. My decision is based on personal reasons. I would appreciate your understanding.

   Regards,

   Anna

2. Hey Susie!

   I hope you're doing well. I want to tell you that I've decided to retire soon. I think this is a good time to retire for me because Mark needs my help.

   Love,

   Anna

3. Basma detested being alone in her rickety old house. She could not stand the smell of the mildew and absolutely hated the spider webs and the dark corners that seemed to be haunting the entire building.

4. Basma loved to spend her free time at home. She marvelled at the excellent craftsmanship in the woodwork and was delighted by the amount of light that made the place feel warm and inviting.

1. ____________________ Language
2. ____________________ Language
3. ____________________ Language
4. ____________________ Language

C. **Choose one of the excerpts from (B) to write a letter or a description using appropriate word choice. You can use the box provided to make a list of words for your writing.**

My Word Choice

My Text

◯ Formal Letter ◯ Positive Description
◯ Informal Letter ◯ Negative Description

My Notes

Section 4
Writing

UNIT 2

Sentence Fluency

The Singing Voice

The human voice is a beautiful musical instrument capable of producing a wide range of sounds. It is complex too, falling into different types: a male voice can be a bass, a baritone, or a tenor; a female voice can be an alto, a mezzo-soprano, or a soprano. If you are lucky, you will even find a rare countertenor (an adult male alto voice) or a contralto (the lowest female singing voice).

Historically, the countertenor was used for men to play female characters on stage at a time when women were not allowed to share the stage with them. Special parts were written for this purpose. Also, young boys were trained to sing instead of females in all-male theatrical productions as their voices are generally higher-pitched than those of adult men. Similarly, women were trained to sing the male's part using the contralto. This voice type is so prized because it ranges as an intermediary between the mezzo-soprano and the tenor. Nowadays, these qualities are appreciated as a form of art.

As you have probably realized by now, each voice type produces a different character. This is called "timbre", varying from being full and rich to sweet and lyrical. For example, you may have heard that some singers are "dark" while others are "bright" – the former is associated with lower-pitched voice types and the latter with higher-pitched ones.

Another interesting point is that some people sing really well at a young age, but it actually takes a long time to polish the singing voice; singers must very patiently train to "master their instrument". The human voice acts like a wind instrument, much like a flute. Thus, students should practise this form of art under the guidance of a trained singer. Some singers say that a good vocal education based on classical techniques serves as the foundation for all styles of singing, whether it is opera, musical theatre, jazz, or pop. Once you learn to support your voice, you will find that you can control your voice to do whatever you want it to do, in any style. Basic techniques and components of singing involve the controlled use of breathing and awareness of the resonance of your voice. This basic foundation of singing serves to keep your voice healthy throughout your lifetime.

Nowadays, people pay high prices to hear the world's most polished voices come together to perform. The next time you are at a choral performance, try to listen for the different shades of sound. You may be surprised at how much you hear!

Also, you could practise singing on your own to see how much you can tell about your own voice.

A. Check to show the features of sentence fluency. Then give examples for the features listed from the text.

Sentence fluency is the way that words and phrases flow within a sentence, and the way sentences sound within a text.

The Features of Sentence Fluency:

1. Sentences begin in different ways.
2. All sentences are short and simple.
3. Run-on sentences are used.
4. Sentences are repetitive.
5. There is a coherent progression of thoughts and ideas.
6. A variety of sentences, including simple, compound, and complex sentences, are used.
7. ✔ A variety of transitional words and phrases are used.

   Example ______________________

8. ✔ Sentences have varying lengths.

   Example ______________________

9. ✔ Sentences contain appositives.

   Example ______________________

10. ✔ Sentences use punctuation for pauses to achieve the desired pace.

   Example ______________________

B. Check to show the sentence with better sentence fluency for each pair.

1. A I met Andy. He is my neighbour. I was mowing the lawn.
   B I met Andy, my neighbour, when I was mowing the lawn.

2. A Julia stored her jewellery behind a stack of juice boxes.
   B Julia kept her jewellery behind some boxes. They were juice boxes.

3. A I bought a necklace for my sister. I wanted to surprise her on her birthday.
   B To surprise my sister on her birthday, I bought her a necklace.

4. A She wanted to come over today. She had to catch up on some work.
   B She wanted to come over today but she had to catch up on some work.

5. A Nobody could tell when Mrs. Hayes would start complaining about something in her life – her hair, her health, her house, or her hamster.
   B Nobody could tell when Mrs. Hayes would start complaining about things like her hair or her health or maybe her house or her hamster.

6. A The snowflakes, sparkling like crystals, melt gently in Diana's hair.
   B The snowflakes are sparkling like crystals and they are also melting in Diana's hair.

7. A Damian's glare was cold. His glare was like cracked ice that rests on top of a blue lake.
   B Damian's glare was cold, like cracked ice on a blue lake.

8. A Cassie did not like strawberry rhubarb pie. Because she did not like strawberry rhubarb pie, she gave it to her little brother.
   B Cassie did not like strawberry rhubarb pie so she gave it to her little brother.

C. **Read the paragraph about Prince Edward Island. Rewrite it to improve sentence fluency.**

Prince Edward Island

Charlottetown

Prince Edward Island was named in honour of Edward, Duke of Kent, in 1799. He was the father of Queen Victoria. Prince Edward Island is the smallest of all the Canadian provinces. Prince Edward Island is the smallest in population. Prince Edward Island's capital city is Charlottetown. Prince Edward Island is located on Canada's east coast. Prince Edward Island gets about 1.2 million visitors every year.

My Notes

Section 4

Writing

UNIT 3 Point of View

At the Police Station

Asam has been taken to the police station as a suspect of a house burglary in his neighbourhood and is being interviewed by Detective Markle. Observing from an adjoining room, an officer sits quietly and fervently takes notes on her notepad.

Detective Markle: Asam, please narrate yesterday's events in order. Then I would like to know your whereabouts after the burglary on 9 Treeline Road took place.

Asam: I did not do anything, Detective! I can explain my presence in Mrs. Lee's house yesterday. I was mowing my lawn when I saw a dented old Honda pull into my neighbour's driveway. You know that I live right across the road from her. That is why I did not think much of it. After about ten minutes, I heard the screech of a car and turned around to see what was going on.

I was able to catch part of the licence plate of the old car – it said 95X. My immediate reaction was to run over to Mrs. Lee's house. As she is an elderly woman living in the huge house by herself, I was just concerned about her and thought I should check. As I entered, I noticed a few things out of order. The front door was open and I found her in her favourite recliner in her living room. She was hysterical and did not know who had ransacked her house!

After this, I was so shocked that the rest of the day seemed like a blur. You have no idea how scary it is when one of your neighbours gets robbed. Can you please tell me why I was brought into the station?

Detective Markle: It is our practice to question everyone at the scene of a crime. I cannot give out any more information at this point. Thank you, Asam.

Officer's Notes:

- The suspect had prior knowledge of and access to the scene of the crime. He failed to recount his activities immediately after the event in question.
- The suspect's body language changed each time the detective asked him a question. Some of the non-verbal gestures include but are not limited to: answering too quickly, fidgeting, constantly looking around the room, lack of eye contact, crossing his arms over his chest, and excessive blinking when he spoke.

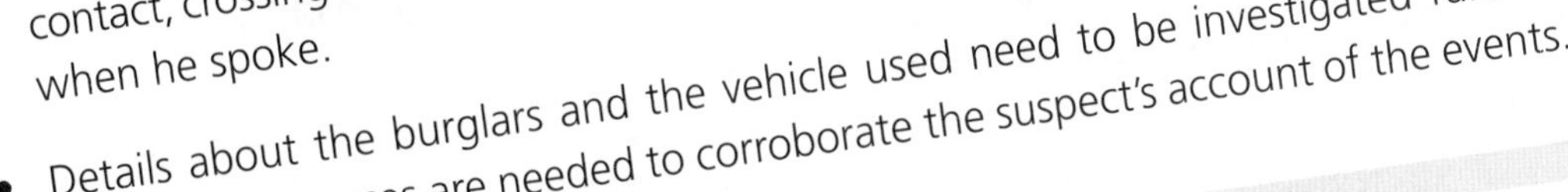

- Details about the burglars and the vehicle used need to be investigated further. More eye witnesses are needed to corroborate the suspect's account of the events.

Point of view is the angle of narration that an author uses to show readers what takes place in a text. It is a way of considering things to show the opinions, feelings, or perspective of the characters. There are three points of view.

A. Read the passage and the examples below. Then write one more example from the passage for each point of view.

First Person Point of View	e.g. <u>I</u> did not do anything, Detective! ________________________ ________________________
Second Person Point of View	e.g. <u>You</u> know that I live right across the road from her. ________________________ ________________________
Third Person Point of View	e.g. The suspect's body language changed each time the detective asked <u>him</u> a question. ________________________ ________________________

First person point of view uses:

- a personal perspective.
- words such as "I", "me", "my", "we", and "us".

Second person point of view uses:

- the perspective of the person or people who are being addressed.
- words such as "you", "your", "yours", and "yourselves".

Third person point of view uses:

- the perspective of an outsider looking in.
- words such as "he", "it", "her", and "them".

Examples

First Person Point of View:

- I cannot stand the smell of garbage.

Second Person Point of View:

- You cannot stand the smell of garbage.

Third Person Point of View:

- She could not stand the smell of garbage.

B. Read the sentences. Then write "first", "second", or "third" to show the points of view.

Points of View

1. You must be interested in gardening because you picked up this book. ____________
2. I felt a sense of responsibility toward my community. ____________
3. They were excited to try out the new ice cream parlour down the street. ____________
4. She could not believe her eyes – the patient was walking on his own! ____________
5. Anorah was not going to let anyone hurt her friends! ____________
6. I tried my best to solve the riddle in time. ____________
7. Sometimes, you need to take a break from your daily routine. ____________
8. It towered above the tallest building. ____________
9. We would like to celebrate today. ____________
10. It came as no surprise to anyone that he refused to tell on his sister. ____________
11. You are the kind of woman who stands up for what she believes in. ____________
12. The more you worry, the unhappier you become. ____________

C. **Pick a topic of your choice and write a short story including two different points of view. Draw an image to go with your story.**

Title

My Notes

UNIT 4

Voice

Dramatic Flair

Natalia and her sister Jade spent their Canada Day barbecue observing their large and diverse family from the sitting room window. Natalia, a theatre and drama student, playfully imitated each of them for Jade, who looked on, amused.

"Okay, guess who I'm going to imitate next." Natalia cleared her throat, flipped her short hair and said in a deliberate high pitch, "Oh, hello, Jade dear, how very lovely it is to see you. I notice you've let your hair grow too long and unruly again. What a shame that is." Natalia flipped her hair again before continuing. "And Jade dear, do mind your elbows on the table. We must try to conduct ourselves as ladies."

"Sorry, Aunt Edith, how irresponsible of me!" Jade answered, laughing. "You certainly have the condescending tone down right," she told Natalia.

"Well, here goes another one," Natalia smirked, and said in a low pitch. "This centuries-old ecological debate is one which has divided many families into the recyclers – those annoyingly sensible people who care about our planet, and the inconsiderates – those who choose to ignore environmental concerns because it's convenient for them," she said in a monotone. "Most people, of course, are happily inconsiderate," Natalia finished, with a straight-face.

"You're imitating Dad!" Jade grinned.

"Yeah. He uses sarcasm to teach us all the important lessons in life." Natalia smiled as she thought about all the wisdom-infused car rides with their dad.

"Alright, future Oscar-winner, let me try imitating someone now." Jade cleared her throat.

"Mom," she mock-whined, "why can't you ever let me do anything fun? I hate it here so much! It's the worst! Jade gets to leave this town and be on her own so why can't I? I'm not a little girl anymore!"

Natalia's face grew red. "I don't sound that whiny and dramatic!" she exclaimed, as Jade laughed. "Let me stick to doing the imitations around here!" Natalia huffed.

A. Read the text. Then write to identify the use of voice in the text.

Voice is set through word choice, sentence fluency, dialogue, tone, pace, and the distinct use of punctuation to show the author's, narrator's, or character's unique style, characteristic speech, thought patterns, and attitudes.

Natalia's Voice **Aunt Edith's Voice** **Author's Voice** **Dad's Voice**

1. ____________________

- descriptive word choice through use of adjectives, adverbs, and verbs
- detached tone
- can be described as objective

2. ____________________

- informal word choice
- use of imperatives
- use of exclamations to show fast pacing
- defensive tone
- can be described as humorous

3. ____________________

- technical word choice
- lengthy sentence structure
- use of dashes and commas for pacing
- sarcastic tone
- can be described as informative

4. ____________________

- formal word choice
- opinionated thought patterns
- use of periods to show pauses and slow pacing
- condescending tone
- can be described as disparaging

B. Complete the information to develop the voice of the characters in a fictional short story that you will write. Draw the characters' facial expressions to show their feelings.

Writers use dialogue to convey characters' voices in a fictional text. The narration can either show the author's own voice or the voices of the characters narrating the events. In non-fiction, the author's voice is usually the only voice used.

Short Story Prompt

Three siblings are lost in a dark forest. They each suggest a way out based on their unique personalities. In the end, they use the most effective strategy and find their way home.

	Sibling 1	Sibling 2	Sibling 3
Name	________	________	________
Age (Gender)	________ ( )	________ ( )	________ ( )
Tone	cheerful, calm, optimistic, reassuring, encouraging	________	________
Sentence Fluency	short, simple sentences	________	________
Pacing	slow	________	________
Word Choice	positive, authoritative, simple words	________	________

C. **Write your short story with the voice set for the characters in (B). Draw an image to go with your story.**

The use of narration and dialogue can show a character's voice.

Title

My Notes

UNIT 5 Revising and Proofreading

Pizza – One of the Most Popular Food Items

Pizza is an oven-baked, flat, round bread usually covered with tomato sauce and various toppings. There are different historical accounts of its probable origin. It has been suggested by historians that the first pizza was made more than 2000 years ago when Roman soldiers added cheese and olive oil to "matzah" – a type of flatbread in Jewish cuisine. Others have suggested that the origin of modern pizza can be traced to "pizzarelle", which were types of Passover cookies eaten by Roman Jews upon returning from the synagogue. Some historians believe that pizza was preceded by a type of flatbread called "panis focacius" made by the Romans. It later took the form of what we know as pizza today when the basic tomato topping was added to it around the late 18th century.

Because it is so popular in many cultures, they have their own stories about pizza. The most famous story about the origin of pizza is recounted by the Italians, as Italy is known as the home of pizza. It is said that on June 11, 1889, to honour the Queen of Italy, Margherita of Savoy, the Neapolitan pizza-maker Raffaele Esposito created the "Pizza Margherita" – a pizza topped with tomatoes, mozzarella, and basil, to represent the national colours of Italy as found on the Italian flag. Since then, the margherita came to be known as one of the most original pizzas.

Another "true" pizza, as claimed by pizza enthusiasts, is the marinara pizza. It is topped with tomatoes, oregano, garlic, and extra virgin olive oil, and is named after "la marinara" – the seaman's wife who prepared this version for her husband after long fishing trips.

Nowadays, there is a wide variety of pizzas classified according to the toppings they have. Pepperoni, onions, sausages, and mushrooms are the most common toppings. The crust of the pizza is usually plain, but some prefer to have it filled with cheese. Others season it with butter, garlic, herbs, spices, or even chili oil.

In Canada, we have our own "Canadian pizza". This pizza has the topping combination of bacon, pepperoni, and mushrooms. In Québec, however, the same topping combination is called "pizza québécoise".

A. Read the text. Then compare it with its unrevised draft below and write the correct letters to identify the strategies used for revising and proofreading it. You may use a letter more than once.

To Revise:	To Proofread – Correct Errors in:
A add/remove words	D grammar
B rearrange sentences	E spelling
C review for facts	F punctuation

Revising and proofreading can organize and refine your writing.

F A A E
Pizza One of the Popular Itims

Pizza is a bread usually covered with some sauce and toppings. (It has been suggested by historians that the first pizza were made more than 3000 years ago when Italian soldiers added cheese and olive oil to matzah – a type of flatbread in Jewish cuisine.) (There are different historical accounts of its probable origin.) Others have suggest that the origin of modern pizza can be tracing back to "pizarele".

The following strategies can be used to revise your work:

- adding information to connect ideas
- removing irrelevant or repeated information
- adding appropriate text features and changing the layout according to the text type
- making changes in word choice and sentence structure to establish the desired voice, tone, and point of view, and to ensure sentence fluency

Example

Before Revising:

A Very Tasty Deli!

Danny's Deli is opening at 9 a.m.

Visit and enjoy the food.

After Revising:

Danny's Delicious Deli!

What: Grand Opening of Danny's Delicious Deli!

When: 9 a.m. Thursday, Aug. 29, 2019

Where: 18 Beaver Rd., ON

All are welcome to enjoy the delicious cuisine at Danny's Delicious Deli!

B. Read the text of a newsletter interview. Then revise it according to the text type.

Our city's soccer celebrity, Andy Anderson, was interviewed by John Rodgers.

"What was your most memorable sports moment?" "When I scored the winning goal of last year's season final." "What would you like to tell the readers?" "Keep going and achieve your dreams." "Thank you for interviewing me." "It was an honour to meet you, Mr. Anderson."

POP SPORTS NEWSLETTER

____
Title

By ______________________________

____

____

____

____

____

____

The following strategies can also be used to proofread your work:

- using capital letters where needed
- making sure the numbering is correct and in order
- eliminating contractions and slang in formal writing

Example

L ~~l~~ist of my favourite things in order from most to le~~ss~~ least favourite ^ :

(1) gadgets

2 (~~3~~) books

(3) movies

I~~'d~~ would like to play video/games as well but they are bad for me.

C. **Proofread using the specified symbols where needed. Then rewrite the text.**

Use These Symbols

X	to cross out
^	to add
/	to add space

Had you been to a iced hotel before? January each year there's one build near Montmorency falls quebec when the temperature is lo enough. come april, and a hotel'll melt Do u think it will be a great ideal to visit the icehotel in quebec this winter.

____

____

____

____

____

My Notes

____

____

____

____

Section 4

Writing

UNIT 6 Rap Poems

Won't Let You Sink

Think what you wanna think

But I ain't gonna blink

When you're blinded by your own bling

Livin' on the brink

You will sink

Not wink

When you run to your shrink

Like a mink

On a skating rink

I will always be there for you.

I will jump in

And kill the sting

So you can be the king

In sync

With things gone extinct

And relink

With the ink

You gotta think

Think

What's the missing link?

A rap poem focuses on the rhythm, rhyme, and musicality of the word flow. It is meant to be spoken rapidly or performed in time to a beat.

The Toronto State of Mind

Y'all, my people
What you waitin' for
It's time to begin
Let's explore
Don't ignore
The Toronto state of mind
Let's play baseball
With 'em all

The rich, the poor
On the rise, on the fall
Don't ignore the call
We gotta empower
Like the CN Tower
We gotta show 'em
What we're made of
Truth
Love
Honesty
Diversity
No more atrocities!

A. Read the two rap poems. Then write the letters to identify the features of the rap poems.

Features of Rap Poetry

- **A rhyme**
- **B simile**
- **C assonance**
- **D free verse**
- **E use of slang**

1. Won't Let You Sink

Like a mink
On a skating rink ◯

In sync
With things gone extinct ◯

You gotta think
Think
What's the missing link? ◯

2. The Toronto State of Mind

Y'all, my people
What you waitin' for ◯

We gotta show 'em
What we're made of
Truth
Love
Honesty ◯

Section 4 Writing

B. Brainstorm ideas for a rap poem that you will write. Then check the features of your rap poem.

MY RAP POEM

Features of My Rap Poem	
specific topic	○
local content	○
use of slang	○
chorus	○
assonance	○
rhythm	○
free verse	○
message/lesson	○
metaphor/simile	○

Here are some tips:

- *Create a hook to capture your audience.*
- *Listen to lively music while writing your rap poem.*

C. **Write a rap poem using your ideas from (B).**

You can memorize your rap poem and perform it to a beat for your family and friends.

Title

My Notes

UNIT 7 Reports

Causes of Decreasing Numbers in the Polar Bear Population

Introduction

The polar bear lives in the Arctic region. It hunts well on land and on the sea ice, as well as in the water. However, due to various factors, its survival has been threatened in recent years.

Polar bears live in the Arctic region.

Physical Appearance

Most polar bears weigh between 300 and 600 kilograms and measure between 1.8 and 2.8 metres in length. Polar bears have thick blubber and fur, which insulates them against the bitter cold.

Habitat and Survival

Although the polar bear can live on coasts and islands in the Arctic region, it spends most of its time on the sea ice. It is well-adapted to its habitat and uses camouflage to hide from its prey.

The polar bear is the most carnivorous member of the bear family. It can live and hunt efficiently on land and in the water. Although it feeds mainly on seals, it also eats birds, rodents, beluga whales, young walruses, and, very occasionally, other polar bears as well.

Causes of Decrease in the Polar Bear Population

- Polar bears use sea ice as a platform to hunt seals, which are the mainstay of their diet. The destruction of their habitat and hunting ground on the Arctic ice due to global warming has led to their classification as a threatened species.
- Consumption of polar bears by other polar bears is a cause for concern. A young cub stays with its mother for about 2.5 years. The chances of its survival are greatly reduced if the mother bear dies and cannot protect it from other polar bears.
- Polar bears have undertaken longer-than-usual swims to find prey because of melting ice flows. As a result, polar bears are spending about 60 percent more energy than in previous years, losing essential fat and being exposed to the risk of drowning.

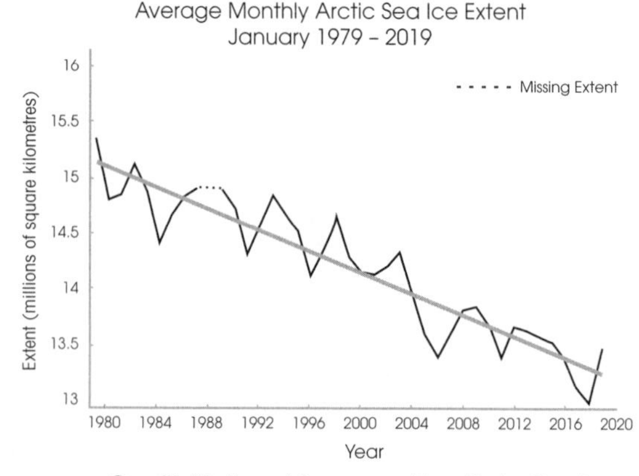

Credit: National Snow and Ice Data Center

The extent of the sea ice has been reducing in recent years.

Conclusion

Although polar bears are well-adapted to Arctic climates and are excellent swimmers, their habitat, diet, and means of survival are being destroyed by global warming, resulting in a decrease in their population.

References

"Arctic Sea Ice News & Analysis: Polar Vortex Breakdown." *National Snow and Ice Data Center*, NSIDC, 5 Feb. 2019, http://nsidc.org/arcticseaicenews/

"Polar Bear." *National Geographic*, National Geographic, 21 Sep. 2018, http://www.nationalgeographic.com/animals/mammals/p/polar-bear/.

A. Read the text. Then check to show the features of the report.

Features of the Report

1. clear objective/purpose ◯
2. informative and factual ◯
3. specific structure ◯
4. figurative language ◯
5. argumentative ◯
6. analysis, cause and effect relationship ◯

A report is an informational text. It provides facts and verified information, using the analyzed results from the data collected through research. It includes visual elements such as maps, tables, and graphs to represent the data.

B. Match the features with their functions.

Features

subheading
bullet point
reference
table/graph

1. ____________ : helps identify the main point of a section
2. ____________ : allows readers to trace the source of information used
3. ____________ : used to make it easy and quick to identify a key point
4. ____________ : used to visually organize information to show patterns and relationships

C. **Select one of the following topics. Then research and write information in the boxes to plan a report that you will write.**

My Report

Remember to include only information relevant to your topic and use bullet points to jot down information.

Topic:

- ☐ Effects of Deforestation in the Amazon
- ☐ Impact of Oil Spills in the Gulf of Mexico
- ☐ Causes of Wildfires in California

Introduction

Data and Facts (Include a map, table, or graph.)

Conclusion

Reference(s)

D. Write a report using the information from (C).

My Report

Remember to include as many features of a report as you can.

My Notes

UNIT 8 Newsletter Interviews

GARNET SECONDARY SCHOOL NEWSLETTER

TEACHER OF THE MONTH
By Adam Cogswell

Recently, Grade 7 student and Student Body president, Adam Cogswell, had the pleasure of interviewing Ms. Simons for this month's issue of the Garnet Secondary School Newsletter. Below is the thought-provoking interview.

Ms. Simons, I would like to congratulate you on being selected as Teacher of the Month by Garnet's Reading Club.

Thank you, Adam! I would also like to thank my students for putting my lessons into practice to enhance their comprehension and English communication skills.

What strategies would you suggest we use to fully understand the academic articles and textbooks that we read?

Don't skip the preface! It usually provides information about the author's objective and perspective, the organization of the book, and how the book is different from other

p. 6

A. Answer the questions.

A newsletter interview addresses topics of interest to the intended audience of the newsletter. The interviewee is asked about their opinions on a specific topic or about their personal experiences.

1. What is the purpose of the interview?

____

____

2. Who is the intended audience?

____

3. Why are some sentences written in bold?

____

similar titles. Once you know the author's objective, it's easier to see the relationships among the facts presented.

It is also important to remember that reading articles often requires more than one pass to grasp difficult concepts. You should always preview the material to be read and skim the table of contents, preface, headings, and conclusions.

That is great advice! My next and last question is about note-taking, which I have heard is an important skill. How should we take notes while reading academic articles?

I would suggest taking brief notes by adding brackets in the margins or underlining minimally. After reading, take more extensive notes. Then re-read what you have jotted down and add more notes based on your reflections. Your goal is to have notes that capture the essence of your reading so that you don't have to go back and re-read.

I am sure we will all benefit from these tips! Thank you for taking out time from your busy schedule to help the students at our school.

You are welcome, Adam. You are doing a great job informing students through the interviews you conduct! I look forward to reading this month's issue of our school's newsletter.

p. 7

B. Check "Do" or "Don't" for the features of a newsletter interview.

		Do	Don't
1.	introduce the interviewee	◯	◯
2.	switch topics frequently	◯	◯
3.	use a question-and-answer format	◯	◯
4.	include direct quotes	◯	◯
5.	stick to a specific topic	◯	◯
6.	ask yes/no questions	◯	◯
7.	include a picture of the interviewee	◯	◯

C. **Pick someone you want to interview. Brainstorm some questions about a specific topic that you would like to ask him or her. Then ask the interviewee and write the answers.**

You can interview a teacher, coach, parent, friend, or relative!

A Newsletter Interview

Title

Introduction: ______________________

Intended Audience: ______________________

Name of Newsletter: ______________________

Main Topic: ______________________

Q & A

Q & A

Q & A

D. **Write a newsletter interview using the information from (C). Then draw the interviewee.**

NEWSLETTER

Title

By ______________________

____

____

____

____

____

____

____

____

____

____

____

____

____

Remember to write the introduction of the interviewee in a clear and informative manner. It is also important to keep your audience in mind as you write.

Picture of interviewee

____

____

____

____

____

____

____

p. ____

My Notes

____

____

____

____

Section 4 Writing

UNIT 9

Board Game Instructions

Volcanoes – The Board Game of the Century!

Objectives:

- Collect the highest number of "boats".
- Avoid the volcanoes and sharks.
- Reach the island at "FINISH".

Instructions

- **Number of Players:** at least two but no more than six
- **Order of Play:** the order of turns is determined before starting.
- **Start of the Game:** the game begins when the first player takes his/her turn. The rest of the players follow.
- **How to Play:** the player rolls the dice and moves his/her "islander" token the number of spaces as shown on the dice. The players take turns until all players reach "FINISH".
- **Collecting Points:** a point is collected when a player lands on a "boat".
- **Penalties and Elimination:** a player moves back one space if he/she lands on a shark. A player is eliminated if he/she lands on a "volcano".
- **End of the Game:** the game ends when all the non-eliminated player(s) reach "FINISH".
- **Winner:** the player who has collected the most points by the time he/she reaches the island wins.

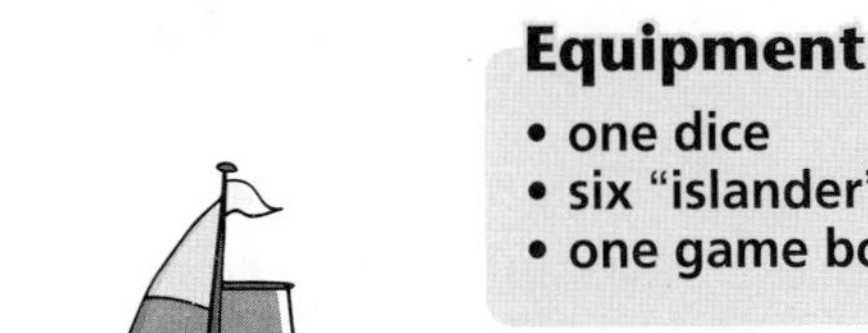

A. Fill in the chart about the board game.

	Feature	Example	Purpose
1.	objective		
2.		one dice	
3.	penalty		
4.			to collect points
5.	illustration	(sailboat picture)	
6.	use of imperatives		
7.	variety of fonts	• "**Equipment**" • "**FINISH**"	

A board game is a graphic text in which a board is used to track the players' positions according to a set of rules.

A board game usually comes with clear and concise instructions that are often written in point form.

B. Brainstorm ideas for a board game that you will design and the information about the game.

My Board Game

Topic: ______________________

Type: ______________________

Theme: ______________________

There are three main types of board games:

- war game – in which the players have to defeat the enemy
- race game – in which the players have to race to reach somewhere
- alignment game – in which the players have to align their tokens a certain way

Objectives

Equipment

Instructions

C. **Design a board game and write the information about it using your ideas from (B). Then draw the equipment for the game.**

Name of the Board Game:

Design of the Board Game:

Objective:

Instructions:

Equipment:

My Notes

Section 4 Writing

UNIT 10

Online Advertisements

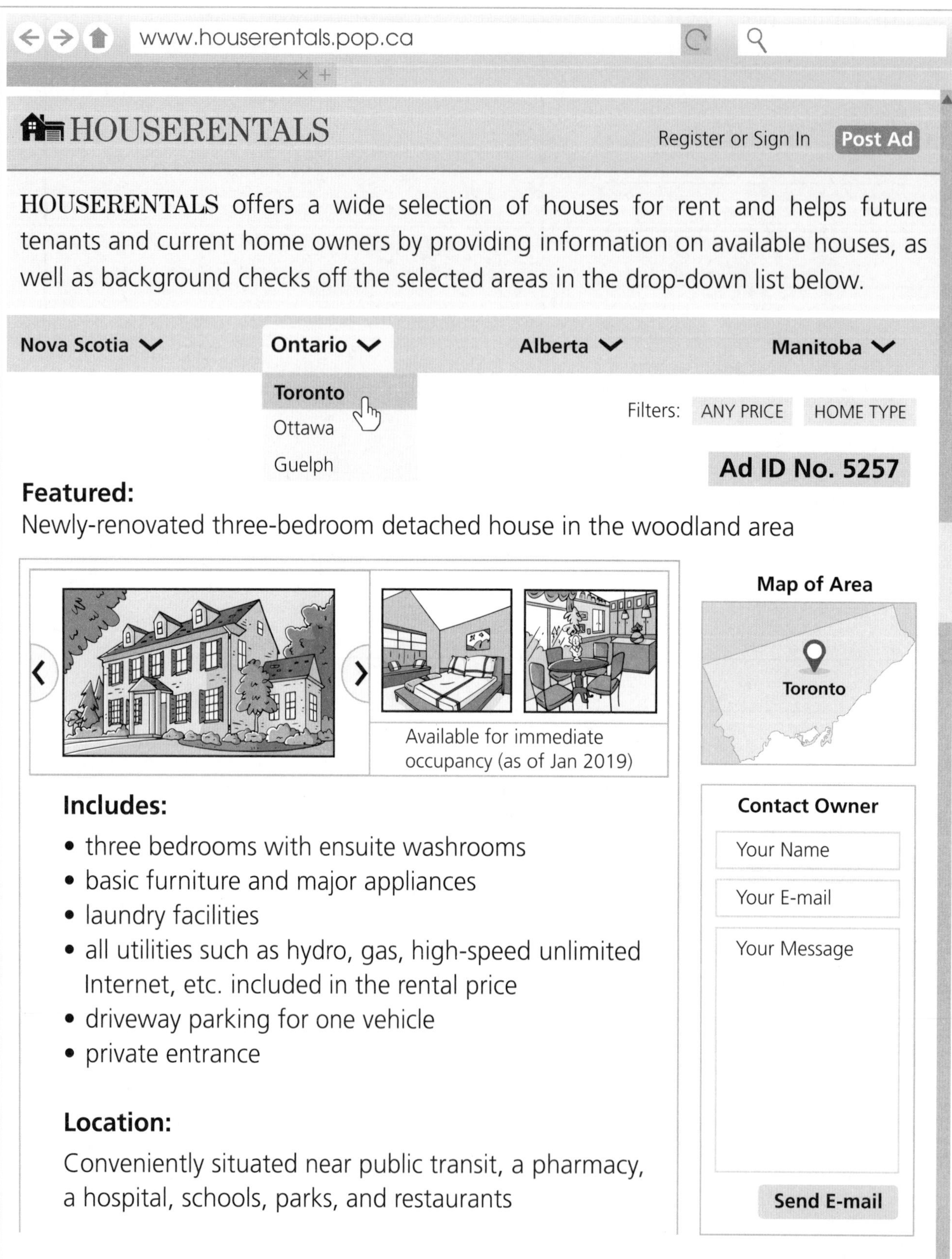

Owner is looking for:

- first and last month's rent
- job confirmation letter
- two letters of reference

To rent:

Please contact 416-XXX-XXXX for further details.
Click to see the postal code.

Read our Safety Tips to make sure your transactions and personal identity remain secure.

SAFETY TIPS

Report Ad | X

SPONSORED ADVERTISEMENT

Townhouses for Rent – Ontario Listings
www.townhouserentals.pop.ca

Register Now!

ABOUT | PROMOTE ADS | POSTING POLICY | LIVE CHAT
CAREERS | TERMS OF USE | PRIVACY POLICY | © 2010 – 2018 HouseRentals Inc.

A. Look at the online advertisement. Then fill in the information.

An online advertisement is used to promote or sell a product, service, business, etc. online. It is mostly used by companies and organizations as a marketing tool and includes interactive features.

Feature	Purpose
ad identification number	to ensure that the correct ad is being referred to

	Feature	Purpose
1.	drop-down menu	________________
2.	filters	________________
3.	map of the area	________________
4.	"Contact Owner" section	________________
5.	safety tips	________________
6.	sponsored ad	________________
7.	live chat	________________

Section 4 Writing

B. Pretend you own a condominium that you would like to rent out. Plan an online advertisement for it.

My Online Advertisement

Website I will post on: ____________________

Featured: Condominium with ____________________
description of condominium

Location: ____________________

Rent: $ ______ ☐ Negotiable ☐ Non-negotiable Ad ID No.: ______

Availability: ____________________

Includes: ____________________

____

____

____

Images:

Images and video clips depict what the item or place looks like and help viewers decide whether or not they want to rent or buy it. Images and video clips also help set the product apart from similar ads.

Video Clip:

____
Title

Looking for:

____

____

____

____
criteria for determining eligibility of tenants

C. **Create an online ad using your ideas from (B).**

Post Ad

Logo

Name of Organization

My Notes

UNIT 11 Blogs

www.blogtforu.pop.ca

ABOUT ME | POSTS | GALLERY | CONTACT US

Oct. 12, 2019

Today's post is about the health benefits of drinking tea.

Health Benefits of Drinking Tea

Although most of us drink tea for the sheer pleasure or relaxation it brings us, drinking tea has also been linked to many health benefits:

- Green tea is the best source of catechins, which prevent oxidation from damaging cells.
- Regular consumption of green and black teas helps reduce the risk of heart disease.
- The antioxidants from green, black, and oolong teas can help block the oxidation of LDL (bad) cholesterol, increase HDL (good) cholesterol, and improve artery function.

Oct 8, 2019

Today's post is about my own tea adventures.

Lessons from My Tea Adventures!

As I sipped my perfectly brewed cup of grainy English Breakfast tea with my friend, I was thinking about the time I visited England to sample different cafés that serve high tea. I discovered that high tea was traditionally served around six

About Me:

Hi, I'm Casey!

After travelling to different parts of the world in search of unique varieties of aromatic teas, I decided to spread my love for tea by bringing information to you through this blog, "T for U". I believe that it takes knowledge, experience, and passion to become a true tea connoisseur.

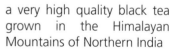

Today's Featured Tea

Darjeeling

a very high quality black tea grown in the Himalayan Mountains of Northern India

in the evening and was accompanied by meat, fish or eggs, cheese, bread and butter, or cake. My friend also told me that although high tea sounds like it was served to the people of higher social classes, it was actually a full dinner for the common people.

Privacy Policy and Disclaimers

This blog accepts forms of sponsorship. However, the owner of this blog is not compensated for the opinions regarding the products mentioned.

Tea Term of the Day

Fannings

a very small size of tea leaf, although larger than "dust" – which is the term used to describe the smallest particles of tea leaf

You can find more information here.

Terms of Use Copyright@www.blogtforu.pop.ca

A. Check the features of the blog "T for U". Then answer the questions.

- ◯ title
- ◯ sidebar
- ◯ logo
- ◯ subheadings
- ◯ live chat
- ◯ site map
- ◯ images
- ◯ website address
- ◯ contact information
- ◯ reverse order posts
- ◯ auto play music
- ◯ social media buttons

A blog is a media text. It is a regularly updated website maintained by an individual or a group of "bloggers".

1. What is the purpose of this blog?

____

2. Would you consider the layout of this blog simple or complicated? Explain.

____

____

3. What is the purpose of including the social media buttons?

____

B. Choose a topic or come up with your own topic. Then plan your blog.

1. Topic Ideas:
   - ◯ Horror Stories
   - ◯ Love of Books
   - ◯ All about Movies
   - ◯ Favourite Foods
   - ◯ Travelling across Canada
   - ◯ ____________________

2. Blog Name: ____________________

3. Heading: ____________________

4. Subheadings: ____________________

Blog Logo

5. Blog Post Ideas

6. Other Features and Their Descriptions:

- ____________________
  ____
- ____________________
  ____
- ____________________
  ____

C. Create a blog using your ideas from (B).

ABOUT ME	POSTS	GALLERY	CONTACT US

Terms of Use Copyright@

My Notes

A. Circle the answers.

1. ______ should be kept in mind in making the proper word choice.

   The punctuation of the text

   The purpose and audience of the text

   The images of the text

2. Word choice refers to the use of ______ by the writer.

   vocabulary

   grammar

   text type

tell/explain

3. ______ sentences should be used to ensure sentence fluency.

   Simple

   Compound

   Simple, compound, and complex

4. Which is a feature of sentence fluency?

   run-on sentences

   transition words and phrases

   repetitive sentences

5. The ______ person point of view uses words such as "I", "my", and "us".

   first

   second

   third

6. The third person point of view uses the ______ .

   personal perspective

   perspective of the person being addressed

   perspective of an outsider looking in

7. What can voice in literature refer to?

   the character's unique style

   the reader's unique thoughts

   the reader's unique attitudes

8. What do writers use to show characters' voices in a fictional text?

   reports

   dialogue

   blogs

9. What can organize and refine your writing?

   rewriting the whole piece

   adding unnecessary information

   revising and proofreading

10. Which strategy can be used to revise your work?

    adding information to connect ideas

    deleting important information

    adding inappropriate text features

11. Which text type is meant to be performed in front of an audience?

a board game

a rap poem

an online advertisement

12. Which is not a feature of a rap poem?

use of slang

setting

a hook

13. A report provides ______ .

verified information to the reader

entertainment to the reader

personal opinions of the writer

14. Which feature of a report allows the reader to trace the sources of information used?

a table or graph

bullet points

references

15. What are some of the features of a newsletter interview?

introduction, byline, and direct quotes

specific topic, writer's opinions, and bullet points

introduction, title, and video clips

16. Whose picture is included in a newsletter interview?

the reader's

the interviewer's

the interviewee's

17. Which text type is a board game?

a literary text

a graphic text

an informational text

18. A board game needs to have ______ .

illustrations and instructions

facts and information

rhyme and rhythm

19. Some features of an online advertisement are ______ .

a drop-down menu and filters

the logo of the company and rhythm

the buyer's contact information and similes

20. A blog does not have ______ .

embedded links

reverse order posts

a postal address

B. Read the text and answer the questions.

Adrian's First Day of School

Adrian was extremely nervous about his first day of school. He had recently moved with his family from Ontario to Vancouver and was not sure how he would adjust there.

That is why, on the morning of September 4, 2018, Adrian could barely hear a single word that his mother said. He only made out parts of it, "You are a very social person...you love going to school...you already know everything they are learning..." and so on.

On the other hand, his dad was more focused on the practical aspects of him going to a new school. He told him, "To get to school, you need to take Bus 81 from outside the gas station across from our house. Then get off at the fifth stop and you will be there!"

His parents' assurances, concerns, and instructions only further confused Adrian as he picked up his backpack, chucked his half-eaten breakfast bar into the trash, and said as a quick goodbye, "Don't worry! I will see you guys at four."

Adrian was able to catch the bus just in time. After getting off at the fifth stop, he was pleasantly surprised to see his new school. The sprawling school campus was nestled between lush green trees and mountains as far as he could see. There stood a state-of-the-art computer centre, a separate sports arena, and even a greenhouse to encourage students to achieve their best.

Adrian felt excited as he stepped into the main building. Once he found the huge, well-lit classroom, he was reassured to see many friendly faces smiling at him as he entered. Before long, the homeroom teacher officially welcomed him into the class by saying, "I would like to introduce our new arrival – Adrian Douglas! He has recently moved to Vancouver and will require your help settling in. I request that you all make him feel at home here."

Adrian was greeted by a round of applause and heart-warming introductions by everyone. He smiled as he thought to himself, *I can't believe I felt so apprehensive about being here.*

After only a few hours, Adrian felt like he had belonged there forever and could not wait to tell his parents all about his amazing day at school.

1. Write two examples for each from the text to identify the specified word choice.

Word Choice for Descriptive Language

Verb	Adjective	Adverb
________	________	________
________	________	________

2. Write two examples for each feature of sentence fluency from the text.

Features of Sentence Fluency

- A variety of transitional words and phrases are used.

  e.g. 1 ________

  2 ________

- Sentences have varying lengths.

  e.g. 1 ________

  2 ________

3. Write an example for each point of view from the text.

Point of View

First Person: ________

Second Person: ________

Third Person: ________

4. Match to identify the use of voice.

Teacher's Voice •	• use of imperatives; practical tone
Dad's Voice •	• formal word choice; welcoming tone
Mom's Voice •	• positive word choice; emotional tone

C. **Pick a topic, brainstorm ideas, and write a rap poem about one aspect of your school. Then check the features of your rap poem.**

Topic Ideas

- ◯ My School Campus
- ◯ My Friends at School
- ◯ My School's Culture
- ◯ My Favourite School Activity

Features of My Rap Poem

- ◯ specific topic
- ◯ local content
- ◯ use of slang
- ◯ chorus
- ◯ assonance
- ◯ rhythm
- ◯ rhyme
- ◯ free verse
- ◯ metaphor/simile

Brainstorming

My Rap Poem

Title

D. Pick someone you would like to interview from your school. Brainstorm questions about a specific topic that you would ask him or her and write the answers given by the interviewee. Then write a newsletter interview.

A Newsletter Interview

Title: ____________________

Intended Audience:

____

Introduction of Interviewee:

____

Main Topic

Question 1: ____________________

____

Question 2: ____________________

____

Newsletter

Title

By ____________________

Draw the interviewee here.

1.1 The Sound of Music

The True Story of Maria and Georg von Trapp

Have you ever watched the musical "The Sound of Music" on television? It is a very romantic and thrilling story – but did you know that it is based on the lives of real people? Maria wrote a book about her family's eventful life, and it was later adapted into a popular Broadway musical by Richard Rodgers and Oscar Hammerstein II. Later, her story went on to become one of the most-watched motion pictures ever, starring Julie Andrews and the Canadian actor Christopher Plummer. Although the film was made more than 50 years ago, it is still as popular as ever.

Maria Augusta Kutschera was born in Austria on January 26, 1905. During World War One, while Captain Georg von Trapp commanded an Austrian submarine and was becoming a decorated soldier, Maria was a student. Before World War One, Captain von Trapp married a woman named Agathe Whitehead. After having seven children together, his wife died of scarlet fever. When one of his daughters grew sick and could not go to school, Maria, who was then a young woman teaching at a nearby Benedictine abbey, was hired to tutor her. The captain fell in love with Maria, and eventually, they married and had three children together. The family formed a musical group, the Trapp Family Singers. In reality, Captain von Trapp's business fortune had been lost in the Great Depression, and so the family was singing in order to earn a living. The group became famous and sang all over Europe.

In 1938, when Hitler annexed Austria, the family left everything behind and fled the country by train to Italy. They eventually emigrated to the United States and settled in Vermont. They continued to sing and became famous again, this time to the delight of audiences in North America. In 1950, the family opened a small ski lodge in Vermont, inspired by their life in the mountains of Salzburg, Austria. In 1983, it was expanded from 27 to 93 rooms. The property includes 2500 acres of cross-country skiing and hiking trails, facilities for tennis, croquet, snowshoeing, sleigh rides, maple sugaring, and of course, music lessons. The Trapp Family Lodge is one of Vermont's most popular tourist attractions.

Captain von Trapp died in 1947, but Maria lived until 1987, dying of heart failure at the age of 82. The Trapp Family Lodge is now managed by Georg and Maria's son Johannes. Several of Maria and Captain von Trapp's grandchildren and great-grandchildren are accomplished musicians and singers in their own right.

1.2

1. How long ago was the film "The Sound of Music" made?
   A. less than 15 years ago
   B. less than 50 years ago
   C. more than 50 years ago
   D. more than 150 years ago

2. Where was Maria born?
   A. in Austria
   B. in America
   C. in Australia
   D. in Italy

3. What was the name of the musical group formed by the von Trapp family?
   A. the Sound of Music
   B. the Singers Trapp Family
   C. the Musical Trapp Family
   D. the Trapp Family Singers

4. What is the family ski lodge called?
   A. the Trapp Family Lodge
   B. the Trapp Ski Lodge
   C. the Vermont Trapp Lodge
   D. the Trapp Family Ski Lodge

2.1 So You Want to Be an Author

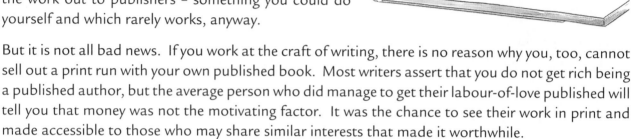

Famous writers are always approached at book-signings by fans wanting tips on how to get published. Some authors (almost always little-known ones) even offer courses on the subject. So-called "agents" will ask for payment to try to get your manuscript sold, but may simply photocopy and mail the work out to publishers – something you could do yourself and which rarely works, anyway.

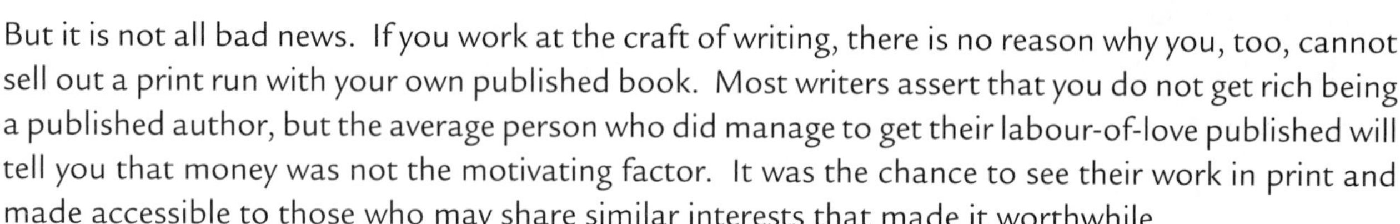

But it is not all bad news. If you work at the craft of writing, there is no reason why you, too, cannot sell out a print run with your own published book. Most writers assert that you do not get rich being a published author, but the average person who did manage to get their labour-of-love published will tell you that money was not the motivating factor. It was the chance to see their work in print and made accessible to those who may share similar interests that made it worthwhile.

With the advent of desktop publishing and the Internet, becoming published is now much more attainable than before. One intriguing development of the digital age is "print-on-demand" (POD) publishing. Through this system, the author pays the costs of design, as well as a fee to the POD company. The book is then produced, using special machines, only if and when it is ordered, thus eliminating the overhead costs associated with warehousing and distribution. The end product may only be a few dollars more expensive than a book published the traditional way (bookstores can also order a POD book). POD books are especially suitable for subject matter that is narrow in scope – such as local histories or family memoirs – but which may still have enough local interest to generate around 3000 purchases (an average first print run).

Any writer who thinks that having their books on bookstore shelves is the end objective obviously does not care if their work is being read. These days, the challenge in becoming an author is not necessarily in securing a publisher, but in being able to sell the book once it is made and to develop creative marketing and distribution channels. Fewer books are being sold in brick-and-mortar bookstores, no matter how hard these shops try to lure customers with coffee and plush furniture. A website and promotional appearances are mandatory. The author needs to promote, and this means establishing relationships with all sorts of organizations.

Whether you write for the fun of it, or want to pass down a story to family and friends, or think you have got something that will make you the next Harry Potter phenomenon – you, too, can be an author. Just don't give up your day job!

2.2

1. What makes publishing more attainable nowadays?
   A. book-signings and marketing
   B. warehousing and distribution
   C. photocopying and desktop publishing
   D. desktop publishing and the Internet

2. How many purchases are considered an average first print run?
   A. around 300
   B. around 1300
   C. around 3000
   D. around 30 000

3. What is the challenge in becoming an author these days?
   A. securing a publisher
   B. selling the book
   C. signing the book
   D. writing the manuscript

4. What do some brick-and-mortar bookstores use to attract customers?
   A. tea and cookies
   B. coffee and plush toys
   C. buffet and plush furniture
   D. coffee and plush furniture

3.1 A Farewell to Pluto

Elementary schoolchildren more than ten years ago learned about the planets in our solar system like you do now. Maybe their parents quizzed them to help them remember the planets before a test. Or maybe they thought of a mnemonic (a memory aid) to help them remember all the planets – like this one:

My **V**ery **E**asy **M**emory **J**ingle **S**eems **U**seful **N**aming **P**lanets.

With this mnemonic, they could remember not only all the planets but also the order of their locations from the Sun: Mercury, Venus, Earth, Mars, Jupiter, Saturn, Uranus, Neptune, and Pluto. But you may have already noticed that this mnemonic no longer works, because in August 2006, the International Astronomical Union (IAU) declared that Pluto was no longer classified as a planet.

Pluto was discovered in 1930 by American astronomer Clyde Tombaugh, and its status as a planet had been debated for quite some time. Over the years, as telescope and space technologies improved, astronomers gained a better understanding of the outer extremities of our solar system. We now know, for example, that Pluto's orbit around the Sun is irregular compared to the other planets'. Moreover, astronomers have discovered several other celestial objects near Pluto that orbit the Sun and are the same size as Pluto. Measurements and pictures obtained from the Hubble Space Telescope show that one celestial body in the region is, in fact, larger than Pluto.

In 2006, when the IAU redefined the meaning of "planet", they created the following stipulations. A planet must: (1) orbit the Sun, (2) be large enough that its gravity pulls it into a relatively spherical shape, and (3) have a "clear neighbourhood" around its orbit. Because of its small size, its irregular orbit around the Sun, and the fact that there were other small celestial bodies near it, Pluto was reclassified as a "dwarf planet" belonging to the Kuiper Belt beyond Neptune. There are now five "dwarf planets" in our solar system – Pluto, Ceres, Eris, Makemake, and Haumea.

When the declaration of Pluto losing its planet status was made, people around the world reacted with nods of acceptance, howls of outrage, and shrugs of indifference.

Recently, scientists have reopened the debate on Pluto's planet status following new research, though it still remains declassified as a planet.

Where do your feelings about the dwarf planet Pluto fit in?

3.2

1. In which year was Pluto discovered?
   A. in 1913
   B. in 1930
   C. in 2006
   D. in 2016

2. Who was Clyde Tombaugh?
   A. an astrologer
   B. an astronaut
   C. an astronomer
   D. a space administrator

3. What did the International Astronomical Union do before reclassifying Pluto in 2006?
   A. invented the Hubble Space Telescope
   B. discovered the dwarf planet Ceres
   C. reclassified the planet Neptune
   D. redefined the meaning of "planet"

4. Pluto is now classified as a "dwarf planet" in the ____ .
   A. Kuiper Belt
   B. Kuiper Cloud
   C. Asteroid Belt
   D. Rings of Jupiter

4.1 The Facts behind the Figures

History may occasionally have twisted facts. The truth sometimes gets lost in time. Below are some famous historical figures who have well-known reputations. But are these reputations deserved? What do you think?

Count Dracula: National hero — or vampire?

There really was a man named Dracula, but he was not a vampire as many people believe because of a book called *Dracula*, written by an Englishman named Bram Stoker in 1897. The real Dracula was named Vlad Dracula (Dracula means "son of the dragon") and he lived more than 500 years ago in what is now Romania. He is considered a national hero there because he helped fight off invading armies. Vlad was not a vampire, but he did like to impale the heads of the soldiers he killed on pikes. Because of this, he is sometimes called Vlad the Impaler, and it is probably this cruel and ruthless act that inspired Bram Stoker to name his vampire Count Dracula.

The Vandals: Wilful destroyers — or a tribe like any other?

Today, we refer to people who destroy property as "vandals", but this word derives from a tribe of people who lived more than 1500 years ago. The Vandals were just one of several nomadic Germanic tribes (others were the Goths, the Visigoths, and the Franks) in Central Europe at the time. But the Vandal tribe were the best fighters; they captured Rome in 455. The Vandal King Gaiseric, who established the Vandal Kingdom, ruled harshly.

Johnny Appleseed: Just a storybook character — or a real man?

Many children know the story of Johnny Appleseed, but they may not realize that it is based on John Chapman, who was born in 1774 in Massachusetts. He was a traveller who explored vast areas of Midwestern land throughout his life. He walked for 50 years, as far as what is now the state of Illinois, planting apple seeds wherever he went. He lived alone, spending time with nature and Native American people, whom he got to know well. He became known as the gentle man who liked to plant apple trees, and so his nickname was born! Even today, you can still find some of the old apple trees planted by John Chapman.

Cleopatra: The most beautiful woman in the world?

Cleopatra was the Egyptian queen responsible for uniting the Egyptian and Roman empires. Some people like to say her success was due to her looks; in movies, Cleopatra is always beautiful. But was she really? A few ancient coins, with her face imprinted on them, are kept safe in museums in England and Egypt. The coins show us that Cleopatra had a big neck and sharp features. We do not know how beautiful she was but we can be sure she was a skilful diplomat. According to the ancient historian Plutarch, Cleopatra had an irresistible charm, and was a good conversationalist. She could also speak several languages. This, of course, made her beauty more than skin deep.

4.2

1. How long ago did Vlad Dracula live?
   A. more than 1500 years ago
   B. about 1000 years ago
   C. more than 500 years ago
   D. about 50 years ago

2. When did the Vandal tribe capture Rome?
   A. in 455
   B. in 1455
   C. in 450
   D. in 415

3. Where was John Chapman born?
   A. in Illinois
   B. in Massachusetts
   C. in Rome
   D. in Romania

4. What accomplishment did Cleopatra achieve?
   A. defeating the Egyptian and Roman empires
   B. conquering England and Egypt
   C. invading Egypt and Rome
   D. uniting the Egyptian and Roman empires

5.1 The Art of Cubism

Are you an artist? Are you interested in art in all, or some, of its forms? It is always interesting to examine the evolution of the various forms of art, as well as innovations in art throughout history. "Cubism" is one such well-known innovation. It started as a new way of painting and went on to influence other artists, such as sculptors, musicians, and even writers!

Cubism began as an idea between two painters in Paris at the beginning of the 20th century – Georges Braque and Pablo Picasso. For decades previously, the art of France was mainly characterized as Impressionist, a style of painting using small brushstrokes with bright and vivid colours, emphasizing the quality of light upon the subject, which was often people in outdoor settings and landscapes. Braque and Picasso wanted to look at objects and people in a different way through their art. It was as if they were deconstructing their subject and re-assembling it in an abstract and fragmented way, usually with an assortment of shapes and angles with very little sense of depth in the picture. The colours were, when compared to the brilliant hues of Impressionism, rather monochromatic and dull.

The term "Cubism" came about in 1908 when a French artist described a painting by Braque as being full of "little cubes". A French art critic overheard this and coined the term in the press. Soon, other artists began experimenting with this interesting style, and a new movement, or "school", in painting was underway. Other artists took Cubism in different directions, and Braque and Picasso themselves developed several distinct phases. Around 1912, Picasso started experimenting with the inclusion of other objects in his paintings, such as chair caning, wood, and newspaper, using glue and paint. We see this today as the beginning of the craft form called "collage", but at the time it was viewed as a significant moment in the evolution of two-dimensional art. Artists would also mix their media: adding shadows using charcoal, using combs to rake through the paint, and sprinkling on sand for added texture.

Cubism in music soon followed, with the development of an avant-garde style of music that sounded somewhat disjointed and irregular. In 1919, the famed composer Igor Stravinsky (who was living in Paris at the time) wrote a Cubist composition called Piano-rag-music, which incorporated popular jazzy Ragtime sounds with darker music inspired by his Russian homeland.

A Cubist style of literature developed among writers living in Paris. Not only did they experiment with grammar and punctuation and non-linear narrative, but they also created written works using postcards, calligraphy, musical notation, and collage. One could say that today's graphic novels, popular among young readers, are a form of Cubist literature. Do you agree?

5.2

1. Who coined the term "Cubism"?
   A. Georges Braque
   B. Pablo Picasso
   C. a French art critic
   D. Igor Stravinsky

2. What did artists use to add texture to their art?
   A. paint
   B. shadows
   C. sprinkles
   D. sand

3. What is Igor Stravinsky's Cubist composition called?
   A. Cubist Symphony
   B. Jazzy Ragtime
   C. Piano-rag-music
   D. Russian Homeland

4. What did the writers in Paris experiment with in the Cubist style of literature?
   A. painting and music
   B. listening and comprehension
   C. reading and writing
   D. grammar and punctuation

R1.1 Ikebana –

The Peaceful Power of Flowers

Flowers can do much to bring peace and tranquility to our stressful lives. They can brighten a room, and one's mood, by their bursts of colour. Moreover, indoor potted plants act as nature's air purifiers, taking in the carbon dioxide we breathe out – in addition to other toxins and pollutants found in stale indoor air – and giving back life-sustaining oxygen. Flower arrangement is becoming an increasingly popular pastime among people who believe in the idea that one's home is their haven.

Ikebana is the Japanese art of flower arrangement. Ikebana – meaning "giving life to flowers" – is an ancient art that was first developed by Buddhist priests in Japan, not long after Buddhism was introduced from China and Korea around the sixth century. It began as a spiritual practice and influenced Japanese arts and culture.

Today, Ikebana is popular among men and women of all ages and walks of life in Japan. As with many ancient arts, different schools emerged over time. The most popular are the classic Ikenobo school, with its simple, clean lines and geometric sense of space; the Ohara school (an offshoot of Ikenobo), which makes use of the plant types that were imported once Japan opened its doors to the West; and Sogetsu, a modern style, which is more creative in terms of colour, materials, and space.

Ikebana is founded on the idea of the essential bond between human beings and nature. As an art, Ikebana attempts to recreate the beauty of outdoor landscapes and bring it indoors. The creative use of various types of plant life and flowers, as well as the receptacles in which they are placed, is a way of reducing the scale of nature in its many forms – rivers, lakes, gardens, and valleys. Thus, in an Ikebana arrangement, a vase fashioned from a bamboo frond is a grove; a single peony is a garden. The act of growing and picking flowers – even choosing them at a flower shop – becomes an integral part of the art, in much the same way as every turn of the teacup is a part of the Japanese tea ceremony.

Ikebana is not just about putting flowers in a vase. It is a spiritual endeavour. The act of focusing on creating a thoughtful arrangement can provide a sense of calm. Communicating with the flowers, and expressing oneself through the beauty of the flowers in nature, can give great peace of mind. It is clear that the study of Ikebana provides plenty of scope for immersing one's self into a satisfying pastime. Those who are keen students of this art will tell you: there is so much to learn from Ikebana – it is a way of living.

R1.2

1. How are indoor potted plants nature's air purifiers?
   A. They take in oxygen and give back carbon dioxide.
   B. They take in carbon dioxide and give back oxygen.
   C. They take in toxins and give back carbon dioxide.
   D. They take in carbon dioxide and give back pollutants.

2. What is Ikebana?
   A. the art of arranging Japanese flowers
   B. the Japanese art of painting flowers
   C. the arrangement of Japanese flower art
   D. the Japanese art of flower arrangement

3. What does Ikebana mean?
   A. living with flowers
   B. giving life with flowers
   C. giving life to flowers
   D. giving flowers to life

4. What are the three most popular schools of Japanese flower arrangement?
   A. Ikebana, Ohara, and Sogetsu
   B. Ikenobo, Ohara, and Sogetsu
   C. Ikenobo, Ikebana, and Ohara
   D. Ikebana, Ikenobo, and Sogetsu

Answers

Answers

Section 1

1 The Sound of Music

A. 1. C
2. B
3. D
4. D

B. 1. C
2. A
3. D
4. A

C. 1. T
2. F
3. F
4. T
5. F
6. T

D. (Suggested answers)

1. Before he married Maria, Captain von Trapp married a woman named Agathe Whitehead and they had seven children together. Captain von Trapp lost his wife to scarlet fever. Also, during WWI, he commanded an Austrian submarine and was a decorated soldier.
2. A. The Great Depression:
   When Captain von Trapp's fortune was lost during the Great Depression, the von Trapp family formed a musical group and sang all over Europe in order to earn a living.
   B. Hitler's annexation of Austria:
   The von Trapp family left everything behind and fled Austria by train to Italy, and eventually emigrated to the United States.
3. The legacy of Georg and Maria von Trapp is the Trapp Family Lodge that is now run by their son Johannes, as well as Maria's book that was adapted into a Broadway musical and, later, the popular film "The Sound of Music". Their great-grandchildren, who are accomplished musicians and singers, are also a significant part of the von Trapp legacy.

E. (Individual summary)

2 So You Want to be an Author

A. 1. D
2. B
3. A
4. B

B. 1. D
2. C
3. B
4. D

C. 1. photocopy ; publishers
2. money
3. design
4. narrow
5. sell
6. brick-and-mortar
7. promote

D. (Suggested answers)

1. Some of the motivating factors for writers who want to publish their books include the chance to see their work in print, and to make it accessible to those who may share similar interests as them.
2. Print-on-demand publishing eliminates overhead costs associated with warehousing and distribution because an author's work is produced, using special machines, only if and when it is ordered, and therefore does not need to be warehoused or distributed.

E. (Individual summary)

3 A Farewell to Pluto

A. 1. D
2. C
3. B
4. C

B. 1. B
2. C
3. D
4. A

C. C ; A ; E ; B ; D

D. 1. (Individual answer)
2. (Suggested answer) Pluto was taken off the list of planets because it no longer met the definition of "planet" due to its small size, its irregular orbit around the Sun, and because of the other small celestial bodies near it.
3. The redefined meaning of "planet" is that it must (1) orbit the sun, (2) be large enough that its gravity pulls it into a relatively spherical shape, and (3) have a "clear neighbourhood" around its orbit.
4. People reacted to the IAU's decision with acceptance, outrage, or indifference.

E. (Individual summary)

4 The Facts behind the Figures

A. 1. A 2. C
3. A 4. C

B. 1. C 2. A
3. B 4. D

C. 1. False 2. True
3. False 4. False
5. False 6. True

D. (Suggested answers)
1. Vlad Dracula is known as a vampire because of the popular book "Dracula" by Bram Stoker. However, Vlad Dracula was sometimes called Vlad the Impaler because of his brutality, and this probably inspired Stoker to name the vampire in his book Count Dracula.
2. The Vandals were a nomadic Germanic tribe of people who lived more than 1500 years ago in central Europe. They were considered the best fighters.
3. Cleopatra's irresistible charm, her skills in diplomacy, and the fact that she was a good conversationalist who spoke several languages, contributed to her reputation as the most beautiful woman in the world.

E. (Individual summary)

5 The Art of Cubism

A. 1. C 2. D
3. A 4. D

B. 1. C 2. D
3. C 4. D

C. (Suggested writing)

Impressionism
- small brushstrokes
- bright and vivid colours
- emphasizes the quality of light upon the subject
- focused on people in outdoor settings and landscapes

Cubism
- deconstructs the subject
- abstract and fragmented representations of subjects
- assortment of shapes and angles
- very little sense of depth
- monochromatic and dull colours

D. (Suggested answers)
1. It developed when Picasso started experimenting with the inclusion of other objects in his paintings – such as chair caning, wood, and newspaper – using glue and paint.
2. Cubist music is an avant-garde style that sounds somewhat disjointed and irregular. For example, Igor Stravinsky's piano composition incorporated popular jazzy Ragtime sounds with darker music inspired by Russia.
3. Cubist literature includes works by writers who lived in Paris at the time and experimented with grammar, punctuation, and non-linear narrative, and created written works using postcards, calligraphy, musical notation, and collage. Today's graphic novels can also be considered as a form of Cubist literature.
4. (Individual answer)

E. (Individual summary)

Review 1

A. 1. air purifiers
   2. haven
   3. Japan
   4. a geometric sense of space
   5. colour, materials, and space
   6. human beings and nature
   7. landscapes
   8. calm

B. 1. B
   2. D
   3. C
   4. B

C. 1. F
   2. F
   3. T
   4. T

D. 1. Buddhism was introduced to Japan from China and Korea around the sixth century.
   2. Ikebana is popular among Japanese men and women of all ages and walks of life.
   3. The Sogetsu school features a modern style of Ikebana.
   4. Ikebana attempts to recreate the beauty of outdoor landscapes and bring it indoors.

E. 1. Sogetsu ; free-styling in terms of colour, materials, and space
   2. Ohara ; uses imported plant types from when Japan opened its doors to the West
   3. Ikenobo ; with a geometric sense of space

F. 1. peony
   2. frond
   3. peace
   4. tranquility
   5. flower arrangement
   6. clean
   7. gardens
   8. landscapes
   9. focusing
   10. calm
   11. art

G. (Suggested answers)
   1. Ikebana attempts to recreate the beauty of the outdoors by reducing the scale of nature in its many forms through the creative arrangement of various types of plants and flowers, as well as the receptacles in which they are placed.
   2. Ikebana is a spiritual endeavour because the act of focusing on creating a thoughtful arrangement can bring a sense of calm. Communicating with the flowers, and expressing oneself through the beauty of the flowers in nature, can give great peace of mind.

H. (Individual summary)

1 Quantifiers and Determiners

A. 1. a large number of
2. A couple of
3. None of
4. a great deal of
5. enough
6. some
7. All of
8. not much
9. several
10. a few
11. A bit of
12. many

Countable Nouns: 1, 2, 3, 7, 9, 10, 12
Uncountable Nouns: 4, 5, 6, 8, 11

B. 1. few
2. a few
3. little
4. a little
5. a few
6. little
7. a few
8. a little
9. Few

C. 1. That ; a ; an ; his
2. This ; His ; the ; an ; the ; a ; this
3. an ; their ; the ; the
4. The ; this ; an ; our ; those ; the

D. 1. Not many
2. One
3. Troy's
4. house's
5. Each
6. Three

2 Perfect Tenses

A. 1. has watched
2. have not slept
3. have not started
4. has broken
5. have not met
6. have not packed
7. have travelled
8. has accused
9. have written
10. has not spoken
11. has melted
12. has fallen
13. has not played
14. has lived

B. 1. (had started)
2. (had not met)
3. (had finished)
4. (had interviewed)
5. (had cooked)
6. (had never seen)

C. 1. (Underline in red): it had snowed earlier that morning
(Underline in blue): They had a snowball fight
2. (Underline in red): she had broken the vase
(Underline in blue): The little girl felt bad
3. (Underline in red): she had not practised enough
(Underline in blue): Laura did not make it to the finals
4. (Underline in red): He had mastered the English language
(Underline in blue): he came to Canada
5. (Underline in red): She had woken up late
(Underline in blue): she did not get to school on time

D. 1. In two weeks, I will have learned how to play this tune.
2. Before he leaves, they will have got everything ready.
3. Lillian will have arrived in Italy by the time we get there.
4. In less than six months, his brother will have achieved his goal.
5. Mr. Silver will have left the office by the time we reach him.
6. They will have mastered the skill once they complete the training.
7. We will have reached our destination before sunset.

E. 1. Present Perfect
2. Future Perfect
3. Past Perfect
(Individual sentences)

3 Noun Phrases

A. 1. the dark tunnel
2. my birthday ; a heart-shaped box
3. My cousin's neighbour ; the collapsed fence
4. a serious car accident
5. the little puppy on the rug
6. the dark and stuffy attic ; his old comics
7. a shortage of food ; the severe flood
8. The scorching sun
9. the frozen river
10. The red brick house
11. a bunch of delicious cookies ; her daughter's friends
12. The tourists ; a quick detour ; their way
13. Her vivid dreams ; her beautiful paintings

B. 1. Dr. Wu appreciated my hand (work) and (determination).
2. I enjoyed watching the spring (rain) by the open (window).
3. Grandma was upset because she lost her walking (stick).
4. Julie said, "I cannot eat the burned (toast)."
5. The fluffy (dog) barked near the fallen (nest).
6. Mrs. Fields is our favourite Math (teacher).
7. We have a strong and beautiful (relationship).

C. (Individual noun phrases)

D. 1. S 2. DO 3. DO 4. OP
5. IO 6. OP 7. IO 8. DO
9. OP 10. S 11. OP 12. DO

E. 1. a glass of milk
2. the haunted house over there
3. her new laptop
4. the crying baby
5. the freshly baked cake

(Individual sentences)

4 Adjective and Adjectival Phrases

A. 1. Adjective Phrase 2. Adjectival Phrase
3. Adjectival Phrase 4. Adjectival Phrase
5. Adjective Phrase 6. Adjectival Phrase
7. Adjective Phrase 8. Adjective Phrase
9. Adjectival Phrase 10. Adjective Phrase

B. 1. The wind blew her (wavy brown) hair when she ran.
2. His (new white) shirt had stains on it.
3. He was (very surprised) to find a chipmunk in the attic.
4. I have never met an artist (more talented than him).
5. They are (truly sorry) about what they have done.
6. I am (quite serious) about what I just suggested.
7. The weather was (not too bad) when we walked our dog.
8. Isabelle is reading a (particularly interesting fantasy) story.

C. 1. up-to-date
2. end-of-season
3. last-minute
4. state-of-the-art
5. well-kept

D. Adjective Phrase:
newly released, extremely dark, unusually strange, extremely excited, very comforting
Adjectival Phrase:
glow-in-the-dark, self-help, easy-to-remember, then-thirty-year-old, brightly-lit, up-to-date

E. 1. small colourful ; Adjective
2. on-the-go ; Adjectival
3. highly motivated ; Adjective
4. do-it-yourself ; Adjectival
5. easy-to-remember ; Adjectival

(Individual sentences)

5 Prepositional Phrases

A. 1. around it
2. by the light of the moon
3. about how he lost weight
4. before leaving
5. in front of her
6. at the nearest theatre
7. on my new dress
8. against littering
9. in my mother's hallway closet ; in Sweden
10. after school
11. on the highest shelf
12. by the campfire

B. 1. through 2. After
3. beyond 4. off
5. with 6. in
7. of

C. 1. with ; the green ; balloons
2. for ; (no modifier) ; when we get hungry
3. without ; (no modifier) ; me
4. After ; a delicious ; dinner
5. Before ; strenuous ; exercise

D. 1. ADJ 2. ADV
3. ADJ 4. ADV
5. ADJ 6. ADJ
7. ADV 8. ADV
9. ADJ 10. ADV
11. ADV 12. ADJ
13. ADV

E. (Individual phrases and circling)

6 Noun and Adverb Clauses

A. 1. ✔ 2.
3. ✔ 4. ✔
5. ✔ 6. ✔
7. 8. ✔
9. ✔ 10.
11. ✔ 12.

B. Subject: 1, 6, 10
Direct Object: 5, 8, 12
Indirect Object: 2
Object of a Preposition: 4, 7, 9
Subject Complement: 3, 11

C. 1. If we do not hurry
2. once the guest of honour arrives
3. because Aiden did not understand it
4. until their mothers came to pick them up
5. as if they had been starving for weeks
6. while you were sleeping
7. whenever I drive across the street you lived on
8. After they had finished breakfast
9. Although he studied a lot
10. Since I am working tonight
11. wherever you are
12. unless you tell them
13. even if he fails again
14. because I hurt my foot

D. 1. (so that he could have some time to rehearse)
2. (Before the coach arrived)
3. (because Matt and Joe misbehaved in class)
4. (If you listen to me)
5. (Wherever he goes)
6. (so that she could remember everything for her test)
7. (once they saw the scarecrow)
8. (Although we seldom see each other now)
9. (Since Peter had never skied before)

Place: 5
Time: 2, 7
Reason: 3, 9
Purpose: 1, 6
Contrast: 8
Condition: 4

7 Relative Clauses

A. 1. (who played the king)
2. (that I bought last month)
3. (whose name was Edgar)
4. (who is a scientist)
5. (that we harvested this year)
6. (whose desk is at the back of the class)
7. (who received this year's award)
8. (when my family came to live in Canada)
9. (which is in Ottawa)
10. (where I was born)
11. (whose son is my neighbour)
12. (that I have wanted for years)

B. 1. that 2. where
3. that 4. who
5. which 6. whom
7. where 8. which
9. that 10. where
11. why 12. when
13. that 14. whose

C. 1. who taught us History last year
2. who taught us History last year
3. who asked me about Tim
4. who asked me about Tim
5. that I had given him for his birthday
6. which I had given him for his birthday
7. which ended on a happy note
8. that Bill told me
9. who mesmerized the audience with her spectacular performance
10. who mesmerized the audience with her spectacular performance

Defining Relative Clause: 2, 3, 5, 8, 9

Non-defining Relative Clause: 1, 4, 6, 7, 10

D. (Individual clauses)

8 Modifiers

A. Adjective: 8

Adjective Phrase: 7, 10

Adjectival Clause: 1, 2

Adverb: 3

Adverb Phrase: 4, 5

Adverbial Clause: 6, 9

B. 1. good ; well ; badly
2. bad ; well ; good ; badly

C. 1. ✔
2. James does not play the piano ~~good~~ well but he is pretty ~~well~~ good with the cello.
3. Mr. Wilkinson does not seem to feel ~~good~~ well today; he looks really pale.
4. The trip was ~~bad~~ badly planned so everyone was upset.
5. Liana admitted that she had made a ~~badly~~ bad mistake.
6. ✔

D. (Suggested answers)
1. Having finished cleaning, I turned on the music.
2.
3. After reviewing her thesis, she found that her argument remained inconclusive.
4. Hoping to be excused, I gave the doctor's note to the manager.
5. Before leaving for work, I played with my cat for a while.
6. Without anything better to do, we thought shopping would be good for us.
7.

E. (Individual writing)

9 Transition Words and Phrases

A. 1. (For example)
2. (Nonetheless)
3. (In the same way)
4. (On the other hand)
5. (In fact)
6. (However)
7. (In other words)
8. (On the contrary)
9. (Moreover)
10. (For instance)

B. Contrast: 11

Addition: 5, 10

Comparison: 1, 12

Example: 2, 4

Emphasis: 8, 9

Conclusion: 3, 6, 7

C. 1. Despite that
2. Eventually
3. In conclusion
4. To repeat
5. Also
6. For that reason

D. (Individual sentences)

E. (Suggested sentences)
1. Sofia was worried about her son's behaviour at school. Also, she was worried about his grades.
2. Kiera loved vegetables. For example, she loved broccoli.
3. Nova was not feeling well on Thursday. As a result, she had to call in sick.
4. This sketch is very detailed. Contrastingly, that sketch is kind of vague.
5. Julian was an ambitious athlete. In addition, he was a great student.
6. The service was extremely poor. Despite that, we had a great time.

10 Introductory Words, Phrases, and Clauses

A. 1. Please 2. Definitely
3. Ugh 4. Suddenly
5. Meanwhile 6. Sorry
7. No 8. Yes
9. Sadly 10. Finally
11. Fortunately

B. 1. An experienced art teacher ; appositive
2. After the storm ; prepositional
3. A spoiled child ; appositive
4. To reach her office on time ; infinitive
5. Having been a nurse ; participial
6. Driving through the green meadows ; participial
7. To guard the barrack ; infinitive
8. Before the applause ; prepositional
9. During the ceremony ; prepositional
10. To make pickled mangoes ; infinitive

C. (Individual clauses)

D. 1. E 2. D
3. J 4. I
5. A 6. B
7. G 8. C
9. F 10. H

11 Punctuation

A. 1. B 2. A
3. B 4. B
5. A

B. 1. ;
2. : ; ;
3. :
4. ;
5. :
6. :
7. ;
8. :

C. 1. B
2. A
3. C

D. 1. The company offered me a good salary **(**$5000/month**)**.
2. National Aeronautics and Space Administration **(**NASA**)** was founded in 1958.
3. The second book was published in Chicago, Illinois **(**see Footnote 5**)**.
4. I did not realize **(**or maybe I did but I did not want to accept it**)** that it had been my fault all along.
5. Which of the following is correct?
(a**)** The green light signals the cars to stop.
(b**)** The red light signals the cars to stop.
(c**)** The yellow light signals the cars to stop.

E. 1. **"**What? You didn't tell me you are moving!**"** Abbie yelled.
2. **"**Her Royal Highness**"** is the movie I am going to watch today.
3. Your **"**smile**"** is not fooling anyone because there is sadness in your eyes.
4. The **"**i**"** in the word **"**igloo**"** is not capitalized because it is a common noun.
5. Please open your books to **"**Laws of the Universe**"** on page 51.
6. The **"**Oompa Loompas**"** were Willy Wonka's latest creation.
7. To form the plural, add **"**es**"** after **"**box**"**.
8. **"**Fragile**"** is an adjective, not a verb.

Review 2

A. 1. both countable and uncountable nouns
2. This ; a
3. present perfect tense
4. will (not) have + past participle of a verb
5. an adverb clause
6. It was a hundred-year-old castle.
7. an adjectival phrase
8. an adjective
9. You can have whatever you want.
10. adverb clause of condition
11. a noun
12. that
13. Interjections
14. However
15. set off direct quotes
16. Parentheses

B. Jade stomped into her room after spending several (CN) hours justifying her obsession with eating a lot of (CN) sugary sweets to her mother. *Why can't Mom just allow me a bit of (UN) freedom?* she mulled as she got ready for bed. The problem was that Jade's mother was a dentist who knew the numerous (CN) effects of tooth decay. She only allowed Jade to have a few (CN) candies a week. However, Jade loved everything (UN) sweet! Also, her mother made her brush and floss regularly and Jade hated both (CN) activities. Furthermore, Jade had convinced herself that the cavities, bacteria, and plaque her mother kept talking about were not real. Therefore, frustrated and angry, Jade went to bed. At least she had her dreams to give her some (UN) peace and happiness.

C. 1. After she had drifted off to sleep, Jade had a very strange dream.
2. Jade has walked into a forest full of sugary sweets in her dream.

D. 1. Noun Phrase Functioning as the
Subject: 1, 13
Direct Object: 10, 15
Indirect Object: 14
Object of a Preposition: 5, 12
2. Prepositional Phrase Functioning as an
Adjective: 18
Adverb: 4, 7, 8, 9, 16, 19
3. Adjective Phrase: 2, 6
Adjectival Phrase: 3, 11, 17

E. 1. as if she had never eaten anything before ; adverb
2. whatever she could get her hands on ; noun
3. because she was so busy feasting ; adverb
4. what would happen to the little town she was destroying ; noun
5. whatever she could not finish ; noun
6. while she ruined their beautiful land ; adverb
7. that Jade had made ; relative
8. that Jade had seen earlier ; relative
9. who was also the town's mayor ; relative

F. Suddenly, Jade started sobbing and could not talk anymore. Finally, she had realized her mistake and was extremely guilty. In fact, she vowed loudly to never eat any sugary sweets again! However, it was not up to Jade to decide her fate.

After much deliberation, the mayor spoke, **"**Although I know why you did this, you will still face the consequences**;** you will be shown the harsh reality of eating too many sugary sweets!**"**

To make her understand, the townspeople held up a mirror and asked Jade to look at her teeth.

"Ugh! What is that on my teeth?**"** Jade shrieked in horror.

"Sadly, those black holes in your teeth are cavities and the yellow stuff is plaque,**"** replied the little mayor.

Eventually, Jade decided to do the following**:** **(**1**)** brush and floss regularly, **(**2**)** eat less sugary food, and **(**3**)** always listen to her mother.

1 Koko's Ingenious Navigation

A. 1. in the Arctic tundra 2. at night
3. a snowmobile 4. a thick fog
5. scared 6. in an urban city

B. 1. sastrugi 2. igloo
3. plain 4. grandpa
5. topography 6. location

C. 1. This is a short story.
2. On their excursion, the girls are surrounded by a thick fog that obscures their vision and they are lost.
3. Koko has confidence because she was trained by her grandpa to always be vigilant and form a close relationship with the land around her.
4. Koko drives her snowmobile along the sastrugi to gauge her location and reach her destination.

D. (Suggested answers)
Similarity:
The small and familiar landmarks of the land are like the stars in the night sky. Both can be joined together by invisible lines to help people determine where they are and navigate where they want to go.
Difference:
The landmarks of the land are joined together by invisible grid lines and cannot be seen all at once by someone navigating on land, while the stars are joined together by invisible straight lines in the night sky and can be viewed in larger groups by someone navigating on land.

2 The Tale of Tal the Titan

A. 1. in Old Langshire 2. a brave warrior
3. fear 4. bandits
5. crops 6. gold
7. frightening 8. a sword

B. 1. ✔ 2. ✔ 3. 4.
5. ✔ 6. ✔ 7. ✔ 8. ✔
9. ✔

C. 1. Tal the Titan is considered a mighty warrior most brave because he fights off frightful enemies, saves everyone, and never cowers in fear.
2. courage ; strength ; nobility
3. (Individual answer)
4. (Suggested answer) Repetition is an important feature of a ballad because it indicates the story's progression and builds suspense. Also, as ballads were traditionally passed down through word of mouth, repetition might have helped the listeners remember the ballad.

D. (Individual writing)

3 Mr. Jones and the Mysterious Noise

A. 1. antiques, paintings, and books
2. They are neighbours.
3. He crawls in through the window of his basement.
4. upstairs
5. on the last step
6. a zoologist

B. 1. F 2. F 3. T 4. F
5. T 6. T 7. T 8. T

C. 1. The protagonist is curious about the strange noise he hears coming from Mr. Jones's house.
2. (Suggested sentences)
"...when I finally turned the light on, I gasped!"
"I walked up the stairs as quietly as I could but then on the last step...the floor beneath my foot creaked!"
"I paused, dead in my tracks, hoping no one was home to hear me."
3. It is either evening or nighttime because the protagonist has to feel around the walls for the light switch.

D. (Suggested answer)
Reason for Mr. Jones's Reaction:
Mr. Jones scoffed at the protagonist's response because it is obvious that the protagonist is lying.
(Individual writing)

4 Johnny's Secret

A. 1. one act and three scenes
   2. Johnny
   3. in the dining room
   4. he starts laughing
   5. supportively
   6. He is embarrassed.

B. 1. Title: Johnny's Secret
   Characters: Johnny, Felix, Mom, and Dad
   Setting: Johnny's house at dinner time and the park
   Conflict:
   (Suggested answer) Johnny has become withdrawn from his family because he has been practising breakdancing and is too embarrassed to tell them.
   Solution:
   (Suggested answer) Johnny's parents have Felix spy on him to figure out why he has become disengaged and they react supportively once they find out.
   Dialogue: (Two individual examples)
   2. (Suggested answers)
   Scene 1: dining table ; plate
   Scene 2: cardboard bushes ; park bench
   Scene 3: sofa ; coffee table
   3. (Individual answer)
   4. (Suggested answer)
   The message of the play is that communication and family support are important. It is better to talk about your feelings than hide them from your family.
   5. (Suggested adjectives)
   quiet ; secretive ; ambitious ; self-conscious

C. (Suggested examples)
   Scene 1: Johnny leaves and the sound of a door slamming shut is heard off-stage.
   Scene 2: Felix runs off while Johnny chases him.
   Scene 3: Everyone exits and the curtains fall.
   (Individual stage directions)

5 My Wonderful Life

A. 1. in Prince Edward Island
   2. Cinnamon
   3. English Literature
   4. annually
   5. writing
   6. Europe
   7. three
   8. coffee

B. 1. This is an autobiography.
   (Suggested answer) One feature is the inclusion of the author's life events in chronological order.
   2. The writer moved to New York to obtain her Bachelor of Arts degree in English Literature.
   3. (Suggested answer) She writes most about her childhood on the farm in Prince Edward Island because she has many fond memories of growing up there with her family and animal friends.

C. (Suggested events)
   Childhood: The writer lived on a farm in Prince Edward Island.
   Middle School: She had a horse named Cinnamon to whom she told her secrets.
   High School: The writer and her sister were home-schooled by their mother.
   University: She studied English Literature in New York.
   Post University: The writer raised two sons.

D. (Suggested examples)
   1. The writer looked forward to collecting freshly laid eggs.
   2. The writer's best friend was a horse.
   3. The writer studied and sketched animals.
   4. The writer had a rooftop garden.
   (Individual writing)

6 Pablo Picasso

A. 1. a professor of art
2. his father
3. He co-founded it.
4. poverty, tragedy, and relationships
5. dyslexia

B. (Suggested answers)
1. Picasso's father influenced his career by providing Picasso with his first formal academic art training in figure drawing and oil painting at a young age.
2. Some of the events include the facts that he started painting when he was 7 and produced his first oil paintings by the age of 13, and that he co-founded the Cubist movement.
3. Picasso did not immediately become successful with his art, as is demonstrated by the fact that he could not sell enough of his works to financially support himself initially.
4. Picasso's first word, "piz, piz" (meaning "pencil"), is significant because he would go on to become one of the most famous artists of the 20th century, and a pencil would be one of his tools.

C. (Suggested examples)
1. Title: Pablo Picasso (1881 – 1973)
2. Subheading: Early Life
3. Illustration: picture of Picasso as a baby
4. Text Box:
graphic box that contains information about Pablo Picasso's family history
5. Variety of Fonts:
the font used for the title and the font used for the speech bubble
6. Variety of Font Sizes:
the font size used for the subheadings and the font size used for the information in point form
7. Short Phrase: "eldest child of the family"

D. (Individual answers)

7 The World's Most Unusual Animals

A. 1. capybara, jerboa, and okapi
2. by ingesting plants and insects
3. rump and hind legs
4. the tomato frog

B. 1. This text is a table.
(Suggested answer) Two additional subheadings could be "Diet" and "Population".
2. The jerboa's powerful legs help it jump up to 3 metres in one leap.
3. The long-nosed chimaera lives in temperate and tropical waters around the world at depths of 200 m to 2000 m.
4. (Individual answer)

C. Animal: Capybara and Okapi
Similarity: live in rainforests
Difference:
the capybara looks like an overgrown guinea pig whereas the okapi looks like a mix between a horse and a zebra
Animal: Jerboa ; Guanaco
Difference: the jerboa has a long tail whereas the guanaco has a short tail
Animal: Okapi ; Guanaco
Difference: the okapi has stripes whereas the guanaco does not

D. Okapi:
- looks like a mix between a horse and a zebra

Long-nosed Chimaera:
- looks like a slimy, scaleless sea creature with a serpent's tail, a shark-like body, and a pointy duck-bill
- has rodent-like teeth

Capybara:
- has partially-webbed feet and a hippo-like body
- looks like an overgrown guinea pig

8 Tooth-in-eye Surgery

A. 1. accidents
   2. cornea
   3. by refracting light
   4. in the patient's cheek
   5. the cornea
   6. several months

B. 1. When opaque scar tissue forms on the cornea due to damage, light cannot pass through it. This obstructs the patient's eyesight.
   2. (Suggested writing)
   Stage 1: In this stage, a patient's canine tooth and some adjoining bone and jaw ligaments are removed and formed into a cube. A hole is then drilled into this cube, and a plastic corneal device is implanted into it. This combination of tooth, bone, ligament, and artificial cornea is called an "optical cylinder". It is placed into the patient's cheek for several months so that human tissue can grow over it.
   Stage 2: In this stage, the damaged eye is cleared of scar tissue and an opening is made in it. The optical cylinder, which is now a piece of living human tissue, is removed from the patient's cheek and implanted into his or her eyeball.

C. (Suggested answers)
   1. Title ; to tell the readers what the text is about
   2. Subheadings ; to organize the steps into stages to make it easy to read and understand
   3. Diagram ; to allow the reader to visualize the information
   4. Numbered Steps ; to break the complex information down into concise steps

D. (Suggested answers)
   Drawbacks of Corneal Transplantation through Organ Donation:
   The drawbacks of a corneal transplant through organ donation are the potential side effects – most notably the fact that it can be rejected by the patient's body.
   Benefits of Tooth-in-eye Surgery:
   The benefits of tooth-in-eye surgery are that the new cornea is made out of the patient's own tooth, bone, and jaw ligaments, as well as his or her own human tissue, which drastically reduces the risk of the implant being rejected by the patient's body.

9 The History of Avian Flu

A. 1. bird flu
   2. 50 to 100 million
   3. H1N1
   4. the "Hong Kong Flu" pandemic
   5. the "Spanish Flu"
   6. disease-control centres

B. (Suggested answers)
   1. The Spanish Flu was so widespread because soldiers were returning home from the war to many different parts of the world, thus carrying the virus far and wide.
   2. Reason 1: Viruses are always mutating, making it difficult for the human body to develop immunity to them.
   Reason 2: The world is becoming more globalized as people travel more and more, which makes it easier to spread viruses.
   3. We can protect ourselves from contracting avian flu by staying away from wild birds, washing our hands thoroughly, disinfecting surfaces where raw and cooked poultry is handled, and cooking poultry at a temperature of at least 70 degrees Celsius to kill the virus.

C. (Check these features.)
   captions
   illustrations
   subheadings
   facts
   source
   (Individual answer)

D. (Suggested answer)
1. The Spanish Flu pandemic killed around 50 to 100 million people between 1918 and 1919.
2. In 1968, the "Hong Kong Flu" pandemic caused 1 to 4 million deaths worldwide.
3. In 1997, the avian flu virus H5N1 infected 18 people and claimed six lives.

E. (Individual answer)

10 Flight Safety Manual

A. 1. a manual
2. buckling your seat belt
3. Section B
4. in overhead compartments
5. locations of emergency exits
6. luggage

B. title – A112 Safety Manual
sections – A, B, C
explanation – "This section shows the steps to follow in case of a lack of oxygen during the flight."
symbol – 
logo –
diagram – Figure 1.1

C. (Suggested answers)
1. Passengers should look at the flight safety manual before takeoff so that they know what to do in case of an emergency during the flight.
2. This diagram shows that airline seats have to be in an upright position in an emergency landing.
3. First, the parent puts on his or her own oxygen mask. Then the parent helps the child put on the oxygen mask. After that, the parent and child both remain calm and breathe in the oxygen.

D. 1. B 2. C 3. F
4. D 5. E 6. A
(Individual drawing and writing)

11 Return of the International Triathlon

A. 1. Return of the International Triathlon
2. in Sydney
3. two
4. 64%
5. on June 22, 2020
6. Get in Gear 2020
7. Downtown Sports Stadium
8. three

B. (Suggested answers)
1. Toronto residents were first asked in a referendum if they would accept the responsibilities of the host city should the opportunity arise, and sixty-four percent accepted. Toronto then bid for the chance to host and was selected.
2. The purpose of Get in Gear 2020 is to provide additional resources and a high-performance program for Canadian athletes and coaches to help Canadian athletes reach the utmost success in 2020.
3. In addition to Get in Gear 2020, Toronto is incorporating a new subway line to better host the influx of athletes and tourists, expanding and upgrading the Downtown Sports Stadium, and forming and recruiting organizations and volunteers to assist with the games.

C. Name of the Newspaper: The Smart Daily News
Date: August 28, 2019
Headline: Return of the International Triathlon
Byline: By Volley Runner
Introduction: 1
Body: 2 ; 3 ; 4
Caption: The Canadian Triathlon Team pledging to win the most gold medals in the 2020 games
Quote: "We will win the most gold medals at the 2020 International Triathlon!"

D. (Individual writing)

Review 3

A. 1. in one sitting
2. four
3. orally
4. no rhyme scheme
5. an uncertain mood
6. performed
7. on stage by actors
8. movements
9. chronological order
10. a graphic organizer
11. decision-making
12. rows and columns
13. dialogue
14. arrows
15. include opinions
16. formal
17. literary
18. instructions
19. current events
20. in columns

B. 1. F 2. T 3. T 4. F
5. T 6. F 7. F 8. T
9. T

C. 1. Dorian believes he is imagining the melody because he does not believe in the ridiculous stories told about the southern sea being haunted by strange sounds and voices.
2. (Suggested answer) skilled ; logical ; stubborn
3. The mermaid lures Dorian and his crew toward the rocks to protect the Lost Treasure of Rastus.
4. (Individual answer)
5. (Individual answer)

D. (Check these features.)
newspaper name
headline
byline
date
columns
quote
image
caption

Dorian ; helmsman ; navigator ; archipelago ; southern ; Rastus ; rock ; formations ; voices ; mermaid ; melody

E. 1. gratefulness ; loyalty ; fierceness
2. repetition
3. (Individual answer)

1 Word Choice

A. 1. (Suggested words)
Verb: mused ; stroll ; enjoy
Adjective: flowery ; breathtaking ; heavenly
Adverb: softly ; absently ; thoughtfully
2. Verb: asked ; has increased ; has been received
Adjective: recent ; international ; technical
Adverb: steadily ; well ; logically

B. (Suggested underlined words or phrases)
1. To Whom It May Concern ; inform ; would appreciate your understanding ; Regards
2. Hey ; you're ; I've ; Love
3. detested ; alone ; rickety ; old ; could not stand ; mildew ; hated ; spider webs ; dark corners ; haunting
4. loved ; home ; marvelled ; excellent ; craftsmanship ; delighted ; light ; warm ; inviting

1. Formal　　2. Informal
3. Negative　　4. Positive

C. (Individual writing)

2 Sentence Fluency

A. 1. ✔
2.
3.
4.
5. ✔
6. ✔
7. (Suggested example) Thus
8. (Suggested example) The human voice acts like a wind instrument, much like a flute. ; Historically, the countertenor was used for men to play female characters on stage at a time when women were not allowed to share the stage with them.
9. (Suggested example) If you are lucky, you will even find a rare countertenor (an adult male alto voice) or a contralto (the lowest female singing voice).
10. (Suggested example) It is complex too, falling into different types: a male voice can be a bass, a baritone, or a tenor; a female voice can be an alto, a mezzo-soprano, or a soprano.

B. 1. B　　2. A
3. B　　4. B
5. A　　6. A
7. B　　8. B

C. (Suggested writing)
Prince Edward Island was named in honour of Queen Victoria's father, Edward, Duke of Kent, in 1799. Located on Canada's east coast, Prince Edward Island is the smallest Canadian province in size and population. Its capital city is Charlottetown and the province gets about 1.2 million visitors every year.

3 Point of View

A. (Suggested examples)
First Person Point of View: I can explain my presence in Mrs. Lee's house yesterday.
Second Person Point of View: You have no idea how scary it is when one of your neighbours gets robbed.
Third Person Point of View: Asam has been taken to the police station as a suspect of a house burglary in his neighbourhood and is being interviewed by Detective Markle.

B. 1. second
2. first
3. third
4. third
5. third
6. first
7. second
8. third
9. first
10. third
11. second
12. second

C. (Individual writing and drawing)

4 Voice

A. 1. Author's Voice
2. Natalia's Voice
3. Dad's Voice
4. Aunt Edith's Voice

B. (Individual writing and drawing)

C. (Individual writing and drawing)

5 Revising and Proofreading

A. **Pizza One of the Popular ltims** (F, A, A, E)

Pizza is a bread usually covered with some sauce and toppings. (It has been suggested by historians that the first pizza were made more than 3000 years ago when Italian soldiers added cheese and olive oil to matzah – a type of flatbread in Jewish cuisine.) (There are different historical accounts of its probable origin.) Others have suggest that the origin of modern pizza can be traceing back to "pizarele".

(Proofreading marks: D A at "a"; A A at "some"; A at "toppings"; D at "were"; C at "3000"; C at "Italian"; F F at "matzah"; B at "(There"; D at "suggest"; D at "traceing"; E at "pizarele")

B. (Suggested revisions)

Title: An Interview with Soccer Celebrity Andy Anderson

By John Rodgers

I recently had the pleasure of interviewing our city's very own soccer celebrity, Andy Anderson. Below are the highlights of the interview.

Mr. Anderson, what was your most memorable sports moment?

When I scored the winning goal of last year's season final.

That was a great moment! What would you like to tell the readers?

Never give up! Keep going and you will achieve your dreams.

It was an honour to meet you, Mr. Anderson.

Thank you for interviewing me.

C. (Suggested revisions)

Hax you been to a icex hotel before? January each year there one builx near Montmorency xalls xuebec when the temperature is lo enough. xome xpril and x hotelx melt Do x think it will be a great ideax to visit the ice/hotel in xuebec this winterx

(Corrections: ve; n; In; ,; is; t; F; ,; Q; w; C; A; ,; the; s; .; you; is; good; Q; ?)

(Suggested writing)

Have you been to an ice hotel before? In January each year, there is one built near Montmorency Falls, Quebec when the temperature is low enough. Come April, the hotel melts. Do you think it is a good idea to visit the ice hotel in Quebec this winter?

6 Rap Poems

A. 1. A/B ; C ; A
2. E ; D

B. (Individual writing)

C. (Individual writing)

7 Reports

A. 1. ✔
2. ✔
3. ✔
4.
5.
6. ✔

B. 1. subheading
2. reference
3. bullet point
4. table/graph

C. (Individual writing)

D. (Individual writing)

8 Newsletter Interviews

A. 1. The purpose of the interview is to congratulate Ms. Simons on being selected as Teacher of the Month, and to share her reading comprehension tips with the students of Garnet Secondary School.
2. The intended audience of the interview is the students of Garnet Secondary School.
3. Some sentences are written in bold to make it clear that the interviewer is speaking.

B. 1. Do
2. Don't
3. Do
4. Do
5. Do
6. Don't
7. Do

C. (Individual writing)

D. (Individual writing and drawing)

9 Board Game Instructions

A. (Suggested answers)
1. Avoid the volcanoes and sharks ; to tell players to avoid getting eliminated
2. equipment ; to determine the number of spaces to move
3. a player moves back one space if he/she lands on a shark ; to make the game dynamic and eventful
4. collecting points ; a point is collected when a player lands on a "boat"
5. to indicate the type of space or event
6. use of imperatives ; Reach the island at "FINISH". ; to instruct players on what to do
7. to showcase different parts of and events in the game

B. (Individual writing)

C. (Individual writing and drawing)

10 Online Advertisements

A. (Suggested answers)
1. to help users locate the information they are looking for
2. to narrow down a search to the most relevant information or options
3. to highlight the area being referred to
4. to provide the contact details of the owner for users who are interested in the product
5. to assist users in taking precautions to protect their identities when using the website
6. to advertise to users based on their recent searches and interests
7. to allow users to share information quickly

B. (Individual writing and drawing)

C. (Individual writing and drawing)

11 Blogs

A. (Check these features.)
title ; images
sidebar ; website address
logo ; contact information
subheadings ; reverse order posts
social media buttons
1. The purpose of this blog is to share information about tea with people around the world.
2. (Individual answer)
3. The purpose of including the social media buttons is to allow readers to connect with the author of the blog on her different social media accounts.

B. (Individual writing and drawing)

C. (Individual writing and drawing)

Review 4

A. 1. The purpose and audience of the text
2. vocabulary
3. Simple, compound, and complex
4. transition words and phrases
5. first
6. perspective of an outsider looking in
7. the character's unique style
8. dialogue
9. revising and proofreading
10. adding information to connect ideas
11. a rap poem
12. setting
13. verified information to the reader
14. references
15. introduction, byline, and direct quotes
16. the interviewee's
17. a graphic text
18. illustrations and instructions
19. a drop-down menu and filters
20. a postal address

B. (Suggested examples)
1. Verb: focused ; chucked
Adjective: nervous ; social
Adverb: extremely ; barely
2. 1: On the other hand
2: Before long
1: His parents' assurances, concerns, and instructions only further confused Adrian as he picked up his backpack, chucked his half-eaten breakfast bar into the trash, and said as a quick goodbye, "Don't worry! I will see you guys at four."
2: Adrian felt excited as he stepped into the main building.
3. First Person: I will see you guys at four.
Second Person: To get to school, you need to take Bus 81 from outside the gas station across from our house.
Third Person: Adrian was extremely nervous about his first day of school.
4. Teacher's Voice – formal word choice; welcoming tone
Dad's Voice – use of imperatives; practical tone
Mom's Voice – positive word choice; emotional tone

C. (Individual writing)

D. (Individual writing and drawing)

Creative Corner

My Planet

Imagine your very own planet! Then have fun creating it through different text types.

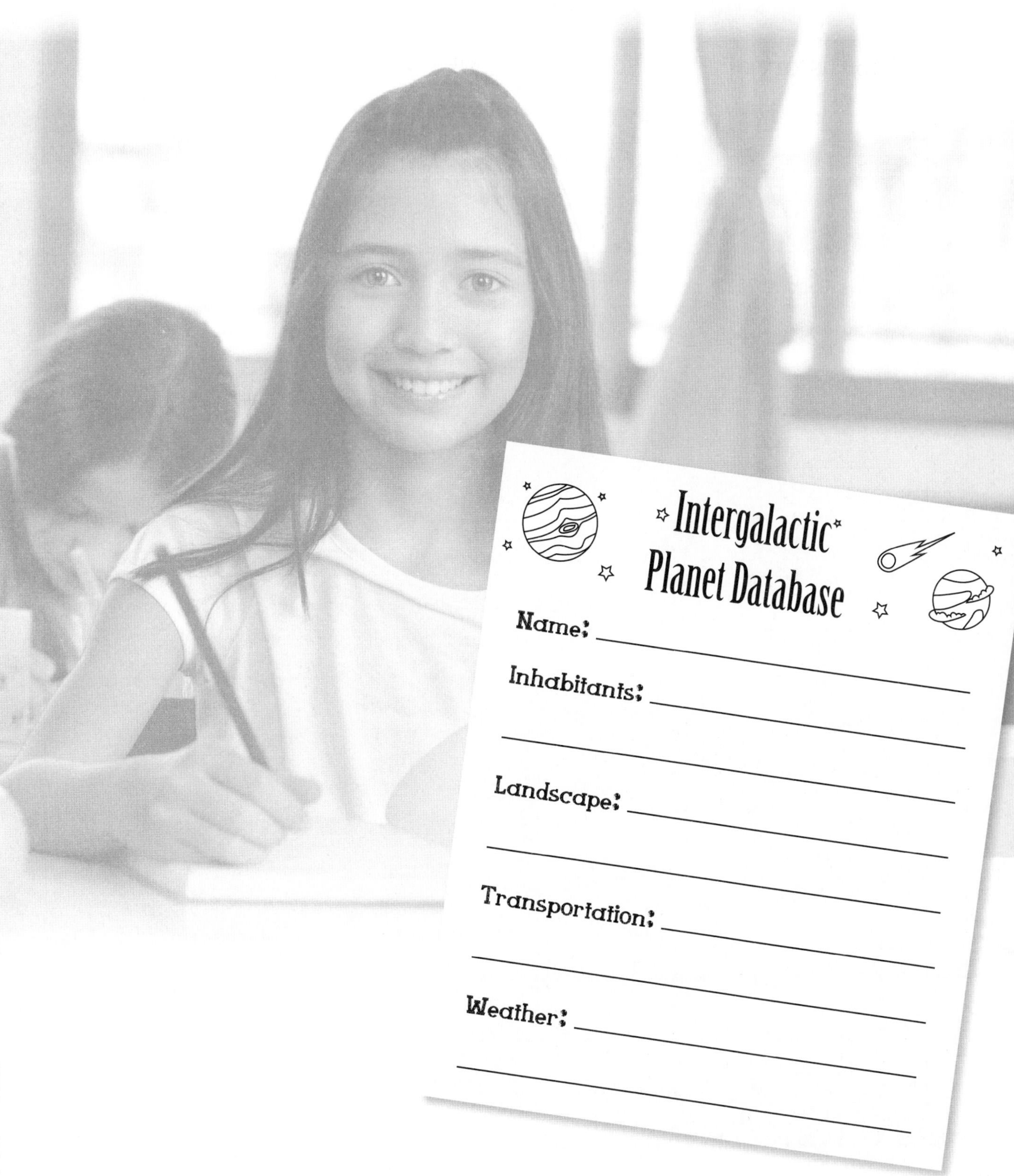

You are a historian of your planet. Write a history text on its origin. You are writing about the past, so remember to use appropriate tenses. Don't forget to use subheadings and add a picture and a caption.

The History of ____________________

You are a zoologist. Use a graphic organizer to classify the different species of animals on your planet. Draw simple pictures of the animals where needed.

Different Species of Animals

Congratulations! You have just been elected as the planet's new leader! Write an autobiography about your life and achievements. Use introductory and transitional words and phrases wherever possible.

The Autobiography of ______________________________

(Draw yourself here.)

CONGRATULATIONS!

There are many different animals and plants on your planet. Create a life cycle diagram of your favourite animal or plant.

Life Cycle of ____________________

Remember to draw, number, label, and explain all the stages.

One day, all the trees and plants on your planet disappeared only to reappear a week later. Write a mystery story explaining your theory behind this strange occurrence. Remember to include the element of suspense in your story.

What happened?

Title: ______________________

You are a meteorologist. Create a graph to show the different temperature changes that happen on your planet throughout one year.

Temperature on Planet ____________________

You are a local journalist. Write an article for your community newspaper about an environmental issue that has plagued your planet.

Name of Newspaper ______ Date ______

______

Title

By ______

______

Caption

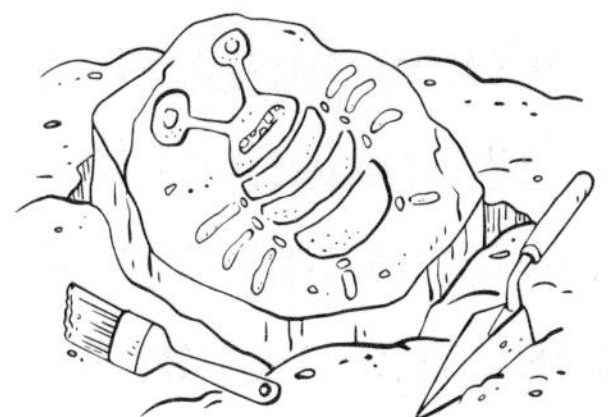

You have just discovered the fossils of a prehistoric creature! Based on your findings, create a timeline to illustrate its life.

Timeline of ______________________

Type of Creature

Remember to use past tenses in the timeline.

Time	Event/Development
	______________________

You are a sports reporter. Write the interview you conducted with the planet's most popular athlete for the readers of the sports magazine. Remember to design an interesting layout and include subheadings, pictures, and the page number.

Name of Magazine

Title

By

You are a fashion blogger. Create a blog post showcasing the fashion style on your planet.

Blog Title

Home

About

Contact

Draw yourself here.

BLOG ARCHIVE

Will more icons and pictures make the blog better?

You have just invented a fascinating gadget. Create an advertisement marketing your invention.

Keep your audience and purpose in mind!